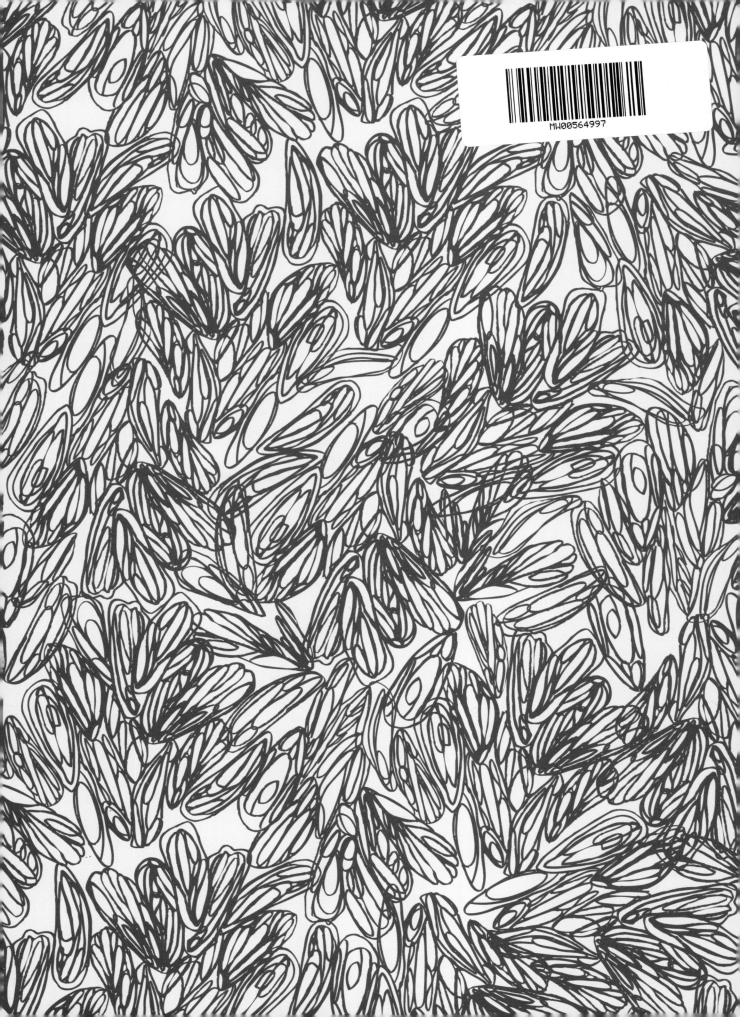

THE SALTWATER TABLE

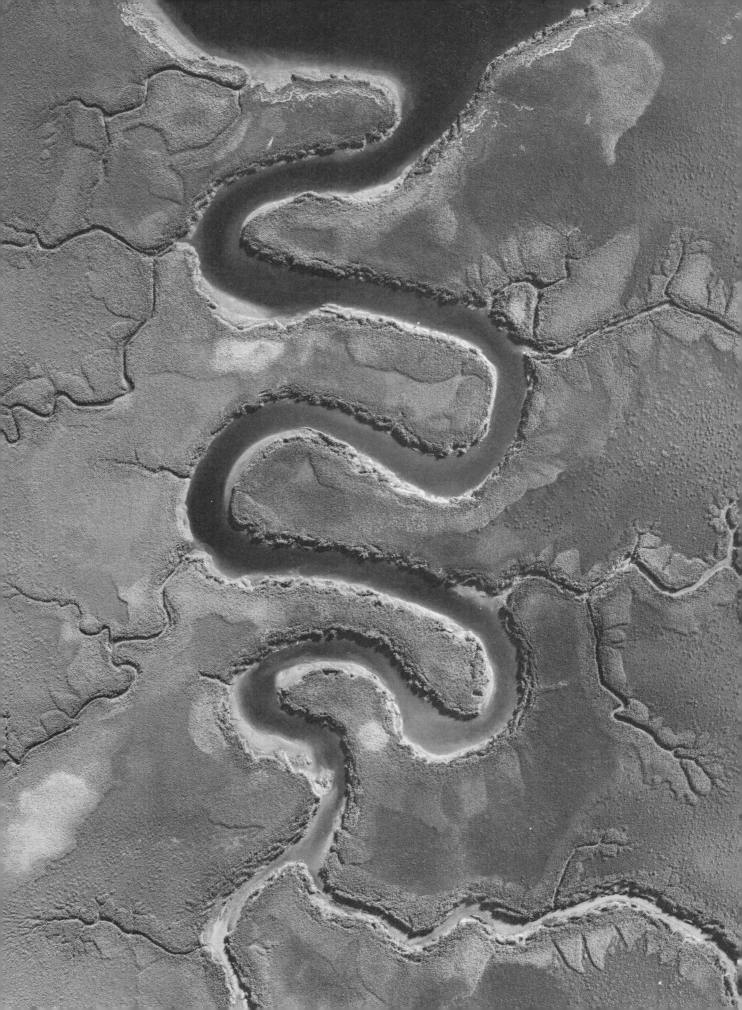

THE SALTWATER TABLE

RECIPES FROM THE COASTAL SOUTH

WHITNEY OTAWKA

PHOTOGRAPHY BY EMILY DORIO

ILLUSTRATIONS AND HAND-LETTERING
BY JESSIE PICKREN WARNER

ABRAMS, NEW YORK

CONTENTS

A Seat at the Saltwater Table

There is no wrong way to set the saltwater table. It's not about one place, or one identity. The saltwater table is about gathering; a shared table where food is an expression of the seasons and the nature that surrounds us. It is where we disengage from the frenetic pace of everyday life and technology and reclaim simplicity. It's a place to slow down and embrace the cultures that inspire us.

Salt is elemental. We all have a touch of salt in our blood. We need salt to survive. We are drawn to the sea, to being close to nature. Go outside. It is where we reset and find balance. Those who continue to travel and learn, for whom the wind whispers and pulls to new adventures, this book is for you.

For Ben, my North Star—where shall we go next?

My Path to the Saltwater Table

IN EARLY SPRING 2015, I found myself staring out at the vast Atlantic Ocean. I had waded out into the choppy current to collect seawater. I wanted to make salt. I scooped cold ocean water into a cumbersome five-gallon bucket. Lugging the heavy buckets of water over the sand dunes was one part culinary experiment and one part therapy. A series of failed restaurants, found love, and cross-country travel had led me to this seashore for the second time in my life. I hadn't planned to be here, but what truly great adventure goes as planned?

I grew up in a small town in the Mojave Desert: Hesperia, California. My early understanding of food combined the eastern European–inspired family traditions that my parents shared with the Mexican American culture of my surroundings in Southern California. At home, our table had rustic *halupki* (cabbage rolls) served in a beer-laden tomato broth, sweet paprika–dusted *halushki* (cabbage and noodles), fried *perogies* speckled with caramelized onions, pleasantly fatty *kielbasa*, and *orechovnik* (walnut roll), generously buttered and served with strong black coffee. At school, kids sold sweet and spicy watermelon candies dusted with chile powder. My after-school treats were *paletas* (ice pops) sold out of a white pushcart with flavors like coconut, guava, and mango. I remember trips to L.A. to the Olvera Street market, where I was overwhelmed by the sights, sounds, and smells of crackling pork skins, toasting chiles, and braised cow tongue being chopped for tacos.

For as long as I can remember, I've wanted to be Indiana Jones. My life decision was proudly proclaimed as I swung on the monkey bars of my grade school playground, "I am going to be an archeologist!" I dreamed of leaving my small town and traveling the world and having great adventures like ones I saw on the big screen. Never once in my youth did the thought of becoming a chef ever cross my mind. It was not that I rejected the idea. I honestly did not know what a chef was. But I knew I wanted to travel and experience new cultures.

After high school I moved to Northern California to study anthropology at the University of California, Berkeley. It was there, in the mecca of farm-to-table dining, that I found myself emboldened by a world of vegetables. I lived across the street from the renowned Berkeley Bowl, where half the store is fresh produce. For the first time in my life, I found myself working in a restaurant kitchen, Toutatis, a Breton-style crêperie, under the watchful eye of its French-born owner, Eric LeRoy. He taught me my first lesson in hospitality, which he extended to not only his guests, but also his staff—the joy of a shared meal. Each night, after we closed the restaurant, Eric would make us dinner. It was transformative. Memorable dishes include La Baleine, a galette filled with nutty raclette cheese, topped with a sunny-side-up egg with a bright orange yolk, and a rustic and hearty ratatouille. The Briou was a decadent galette of melted brie folded into a crisp, buttery buckwheat shell and topped with fresh basil and garlic-infused crème fraîche. A new path to exploring the world was being introduced to me. I was cooking and learning the nuanced work of restaurants surrounded by some of the best food in the country. Unbeknownst to me, I was becoming a chef.

In 2005, I moved across the country to Georgia. I knew nothing about southern food, but this is where my love affair with cooking really took off. The land in the South is fertile. Agriculture is visible every day, especially in a small town like Athens. You can drive fifteen minutes out of town and you are in the country with lush fields and hundred-year-old barns falling in, overgrown by kudzu. The past is always present—on the plate, in the field, and in the people you meet. This is the South I was introduced to and fell in love with. I became inspired by the complex history and traditions of southern cooking, and I decided to immerse myself.

In search of the best education I could find, I landed a job at Five & Ten working for Chef Hugh Acheson. For the first time, I was in a restaurant that worked directly with farmers. Brown, white, and speckled eggs with small feathers affixed to the shell were ushered in. A parade of plump juicy tomatoes, spicy arugula, white-washed hakurei turnips, peppery blackberries, sweet warm strawberries, full healthy heads of cabbage, and bright green okra. These ingredients were dropped off at the back door of the restaurant and I washed them, prepped them, cooked them, and coveted them. Grits, collard greens, chicken bog, shrimp pilau, hoppin' john, pimento

cheese—it was a rapid and glorious introduction to southern food. I was cooking seven days a week, twelve to fourteen hours a day. I cooked alongside my best friend and, unknown to me at the time, my future husband, Ben Wheatley.

Ben added to the sweeping romance of my culinary exploration of the South. I was learning about traditional ingredients and favored dishes from a restaurant perspective, but it was the family traditions that Ben shared with me that made a lasting impact on my southern education—warm cracklin' cornbread with soupy braised turnip greens; tooth-achingly sweet caramel cake, delicately layered; whole hog barbecue; and his papa's stew. It's the dishes you find in a home that can teach you the most about a place and its ingredients.

While studying the foodways of the South, I also pushed myself in new directions and set off on new adventures. I knew that to be a well-rounded chef I needed to pursue a culinary education in as many kitchens as I could get into. I staged at Le Bernardin and Per Se in New York City. At Dan Barber's world-famous Stone Barns at Blue Hill, I worked in the kitchen, explored the farms, and ate a meal that changed my perspective on farm-to-table dining. These explorations left me inspired and determined to perpetuate the shared ethos of these restaurants, a respect for the best ingredients and an emphatic expression of place.

In 2010, I knew it was time to venture out on my own. I was ready to cook dishes that were a reflection of who I am, my inspirations and my influences. As I daydreamed of how I would get to this next step, Cumberland Island presented itself—a chef I was working for mentioned it in passing. It was not a well-known culinary destination at the time; oddly enough I had learned about it years earlier watching a PBS special about national parks. Cumberland Island is a remote barrier island, a national seashore off the coast of Georgia. Most who see the island see wild beauty and undeveloped coastline. I saw the opportunity to create a truly unique culinary program. Hidden away on this island sits a sixteen-room inn, Greyfield, with a two-acre organic garden and access to the undeveloped seventeen-mile-long island that surrounds it. I wrote a letter to the proprietors of Greyfield proposing that they appoint me as their chef. I visited the island, cooked a dinner for the guests, and I was hired—as simple as that. Ben and I sold almost everything we owned and we moved to this protected national seashore with a permanent population of around forty-five people.

On Cumberland Island Ben and I quickly learned that cooking is not confined to the kitchen. There are wood grills and smokers, with stacks of freshly chopped cedar and oak ready to be burned down into coals. The intracoastal waterway is visible from the kitchen window—shrimp and fishing boats can be seen passing by daily. Outside we collected bay leaves, fig leaves, wild mushrooms, muscadines, and wild blueberries. Citrus trees are prolific and wild banana trees are rooted in a marshy corner of the garden. The honey produced by the numerous beehives on the island is a golden elixir with a unique cinnamon quality. Wild pigs root around and grow fat on acorns in the fall, and deer can frequently be seen in the maritime forest. This island begs to be explored. Ben and I spent our days off roaming the nearly deserted beaches and long-forgotten trails that wind through the island's dense palmettos and ancient oaks. For any chef, it is a unique and rare opportunity to cook and create in such close proximity to the ingredients that drive the cuisine. I made it my mission to showcase what was so incredibly special about this island and its place in the culinary landscape of the southeastern coast.

But as fate would have it, my first move to the island was short lived. In my first year of working on Cumberland Island, I was offered the opportunity to join the cast of *Top Chef*. I knew that I had to accept. But I struggled. I struggled to find who I was in the food I was cooking. You can be an amazing cook working for years under another chef, but that doesn't make you a chef, it doesn't give you a vision. I needed to find confidence in my own cooking style. I left the island after I filmed the show to start that journey. I worked with small farms and local southern producers as the chef of a restaurant, Farm 255, whose focus was hyper-locality. I had the opportunity to travel to Oaxaca and Mexico City to study the techniques and flavors of Mexican cuisine as the chef of Cinco y Diez, which forever changed the way that I cook. But at the end of this journey of discovery, I stood again at a crossroads. Without warning Cinco y Diez had shuttered. There were signs pointing to Atlanta, Miami, and New York but I was lost.

I stood still for a moment and realized that I needed to go back. Back to the place that I was drawn to when I first took the helm as chef, to a job I had not completed. On Cumberland, the culinary program sat like a lump of clay, waiting to be shaped. It was a story that needed to be told, a fertile culinary landscape that was more than the stereotype of southern cooking. It's a place that reflects Caribbean, West African, Spanish, and English ties. It is home to a rich agricultural community and abundant seafood. It is the South that I wanted to share. I wanted to go back to Cumberland, to the place that had nurtured my creativity and had shown me the importance of nature and finding balance. Back to the salt.

And that's how I found myself knee-deep in the Atlantic waves. Learning to make salt from the sea and ultimately cooking the food I set out to create five years earlier. I took that salt water, settled it to separate any impurities and sand, strained it into shallow tubs, and patiently let the sun dehydrate it into salt. A storm blew through and diluted half of my experiment. I battled sand gnats and mosquitos, using cheesecloth to protect my salt water. In six weeks, I had big fat salt crystals from the sea. With my renewed confidence, I began to see the island as my teacher, using what was around me to cook and explore.

The truth of the matter is that I never really stopped my childhood pursuit to become Indiana Jones. Being a chef and exploring culinary traditions became my life's journey. My adventures have taken me to Teotitlán del Valle, Mexico, where I poured mezcal in a graveyard for locals during the celebration of Día de Los Muertos. I chose a three-hour detour in France to Isigny-sur-Mer in order to taste the famed butter and eat the best croissant of my life. Learning from famed Spanish winemaker Raul Perez meant little sleep but the chance to explore dozens of vineyards across Spain and Portugal and the reward of a bottle of 1963 Port. Living and cooking on Cumberland Island taught me the importance of getting off the beaten path to find inspiration and seek out authenticity. It is on this wild island that the story of my cooking really took shape, a place where I could bring my surroundings to the table. I carry this lesson with me every day in the kitchen and when I travel to new destinations.

There will never be a day when I stop learning all I can about cooking. My goal is to continue to show and teach others about food through travel and culture. This book is my shared adventure with you—a reflection of the South that I have explored. This is *The Saltwater Table*.

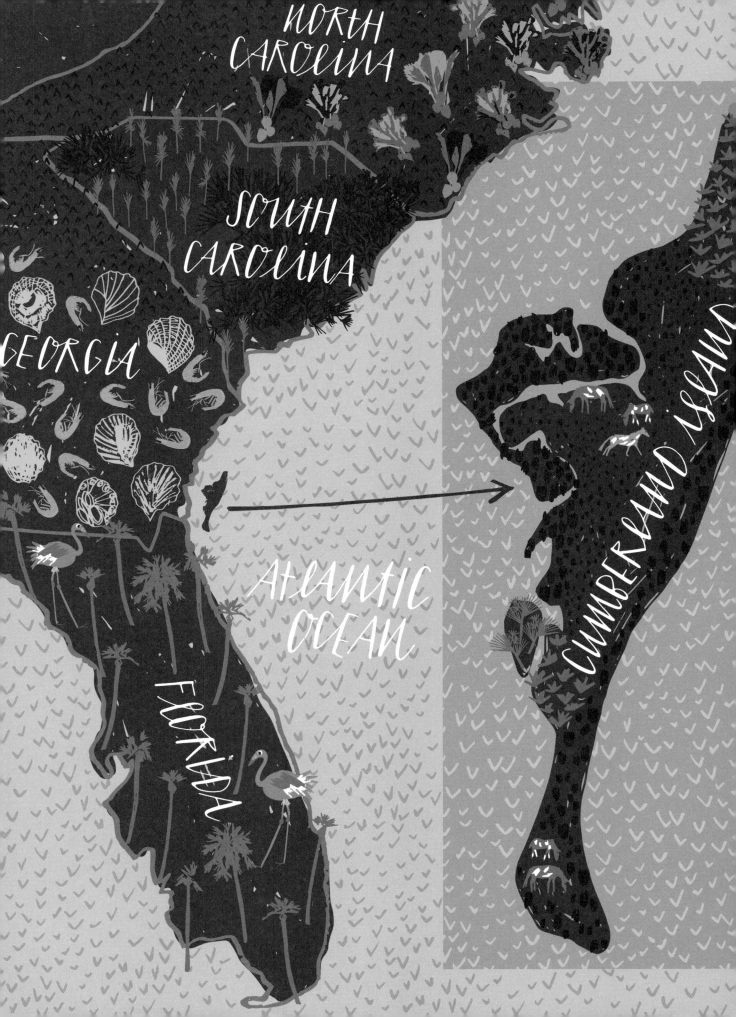

The Marsh, the Land, and the Sea: The Southeast Coast

The South Atlantic Coastal Plain is a geographic region that characterizes the Atlantic coasts of Florida, Georgia, and the Carolinas. The Gulf Stream transports the warm, rich waters of the Atlantic along the coast. The westerly breezes of the Caribbean dance along the sand dunes and weave through the gnarled oaks and palmettos of ancient maritime forests. This is a region of constant movement, where tides and wind control the course of the day. It is a landscape of endless rivers that twist and coil through rich, muddy marshes that push out into the Atlantic Ocean. The lush coastal salt marsh ecosystem supports an abundant population of shrimp, crabs, and fish. Oyster reefs rise up from the pluff mud, and clams burrow deep down out of sight. In the sandy soil, glasswort and saw palmetto freely grow wild. Cultivated rice, sugarcane, blueberries, and citrus trees thrive in the warm climate and abundant rainfall.

The southern coast is dotted with barrier islands. Geographically they sit removed from the mainland, with many left minimally developed. There is a feeling of solitude and respite in this environment whose isolated nature has protected the ecology and the secrets of its history. Rumors abound that legendary pirate Blackbeard buried his treasure on the Georgia coast, while deep in the Atlantic waters lay the bones of sunken ships weighted with forgotten treasure. The fields of Sea Island cotton and indigo that once supported the plantation economy have long since disappeared, replaced by fields of wild brush and palmettos. The past is always present in this part of the South.

This region has been shaped by multicultural influence, iconic historic foodways, and migration of new communities. Low Country cuisine, extending from the Carolinas to northeast Florida, is rooted in history. Ingredients like okra, watermelon, black-eyed peas, and benne seeds were carried across the Atlantic by West African slaves. The coast is home to their descendants, the Gullah and Geechee communities, who carry on the food traditions that are the foundation of some of the South's most iconic dishes. The southeast is also influenced by its close proximity to the Caribbean. Cuban, Puerto Rican, and Haitian communities continue to help

define the flavors of the region, a place where lemongrass and tropical fruits grow abundantly. From the sea to the rich agricultural communities, the flavors of this region have a unique and distinct story to share.

CUMBERLAND ISLAND

Cumberland Island is the southernmost and largest of Georgia's barrier islands at seventeen miles long. In 1972, it was designated a national seashore and for that reason Cumberland Island looks much as it did three hundred years ago. The history of Cumberland is a story of occupation, war, and preservation. It has played host to many inhabitants. The island was settled by the indigenous Timucua, who lived in what is now North Florida. Spanish missionaries and explorers came to the island in the mid-1500s, christening it San Pedro and leaving behind the wild horses and pigs that still roam the island today. Over a two-hundred-year period, the Spanish, English, and French would attempt to occupy and dominate the island. James Oglethorpe renamed the island for Prince William, Duke of Cumberland. After the Revolutionary War, a succession of landowners would cultivate the island, establish plantations, and enforce an era of slavery. Forests were cleared, and fields of Sea Island cotton, citrus, and indigo were grown.

The Civil War brought sweeping change to Cumberland and a new legacy that would shape her modern history. In the late 1800s, former slaves of Stafford plantation purchased land and established the Half Moon Bluff community, whose residents lived on the island until the mid-1960s. They built the First African Baptist Church, today an iconic image of Cumberland. The mild winters of the region attracted business luminaries from the North. The Rockefellers, Vanderbilts, and Morgans began to flock to the southeast coast, bringing their own expectations of a refined, urban life to the lush vibrancy of the region. Falling under the spell of Cumberland Island, Thomas and Lucy Carnegie would come to acquire 90 percent of the land, building the elegant mansions known as Dungeness, Greyfield, Plum Orchard, the Grange, the Cottage, and Stafford House. Their formal hospitality is reflected in their architectural contributions to the island as well as their love of a shared table and lavish entertainment. A new era of the aristocratic bohemian was born.

The lavish island life would succumb to the depression-era economy of the 1930s. Owing to the cost of their upkeep, the extravagant houses once filled with Gatsby-esque parties sat silent and heavy, falling into disrepair. However, their deep connection to the land was inescapable, and the Carnegie heirs sought to preserve the island. In the late 1960s, the threat of land development would reroute the island's history. The heirs of these homes, who had long acted as stewards of the land, sought to conserve and protect Cumberland. In 1972, they donated the majority of the

Island as a national seashore, preserving its pristine environment for future generations. Today, the National Park Service provides public access to the island, limiting the number of daily visitors in order to make minimal impact on the environment. Small parcels of land are still held by private landowners, inherited over generations, who continue to preserve and protect this wild landscape. There are no bridges that will take you to Cumberland. Travel by boat is the only way to reach her shores.

Layer upon layer, century upon century, the history and the people that have called Cumberland home have sculpted a truly unique place. It is this wild, isolated nature that over centuries added to its lore, drawing in travelers and artists. Cumberland Island is a place where the Kennedys have hosted secret weddings, and Baryshnikov has danced on empty beaches. The island's rustic beauty is graced with a touch of magic, where time seems to stand still. Experiencing the island is transcendent. It is salt and sweat. It is the pervasive cacophony of cicadas in the summer, the smell of oak and cedar burning in a hundred-year-old fireplace, leather chairs cracked with age, magnificent rugs worn by family visits and welcomed travelers. It is alligator skulls, fossilized sharks' teeth, the sound of horses' hooves pounding on oyster shell–lined paths. It is the rustling of Spanish moss that drips from three-hundred-year-old oak trees and loggerhead turtles nesting in pristine sand dunes under a starlit sky. Spanish coins lay just beneath the surface of the sandy pathways, a reminder that the past is never far behind.

GREYFIELD

As a traveler to Cumberland Island there are two ways to arrive: as a visitor with the national park system or as a guest at Greyfield, the hundred-year-old property converted into an inn, still owned and operated by the descendants of Thomas Carnegie. With only sixteen rooms, this small inn is a refuge from the world. No internet connection, no paved roads, no traffic, no stores. It is a place to get lost in nature.

While Cumberland played host to my many adventures, Greyfield is where I was able to bring the natural elements that surrounded me to the plate. The ingredients would reveal themselves and inspire the food. Sometimes it was eighteen glossy-eyed, bright-fuchsia vermillion snappers brought to the dock by a local fisherman. On a walk in the forest, an oversize chicken of the woods mushroom would fan out from a tree trunk, begging to be slow roasted for the night's dinner. Occasionally the gardeners would bring in hundreds of perfectly sweet baby Mokum carrots because they needed to clear the bed for the next crop. The island would dictate what needed to be cooked and I was happy to translate.

Gathered around a communal table, guests indulged my need to create. I shared the dishes that reflected my interpretations of the ingredients and cultures around me. For me, the heart of any home is the kitchen. For me, Greyfield was home.

Welcome to the Tropical South: The Seasons and This Book

To be a chef is to be a student of history. The crops that are cultivated, the techniques in which they are cooked, and the methods of preservation are all a part of a larger story. When I cook, I draw upon this history. The tropical South is a convergence of cultural influences that is shaping a new narrative in southern cooking, inclusive of the generations that have come before and the new communities emerging.

Many of the dishes in this book draw upon the influences of the region that I have been lucky enough to experience. Low Country cooking inspired my version of chili made with Sea Island red peas (page 250) and is the inspiration for my Fish, Shrimp, and Grits (page 267). Caribbean flavors can be seen in dishes like Grilled Coconut Chicken (see opposite page and page 144) and Slow-Braised Pork Shoulder (page 263). The story of Florida's cuisine is too often left out of the conversation of southern food, when it should be ushered in whole-heartedly. Mangos are as much a part of this region as collard greens. In the tropical South, citrus-spiked marinades, smoked fish, and hot peppers adorn the plate.

Produce plays a strong role in southern cuisine and has a huge impact on how I cook. Learning to cook in California taught me the value of good produce, a state that has access to a year-round growing season, and its mantra for good food is quality and simplicity. The South has a similar drive for seasonality, but the growing seasons are cyclical, which has instilled the need for preservation. Under my watch, southern vegetables are cooked gently, retaining crunch and texture. Butter and pork fat can be exchanged for olive oil and dried chiles. I want you to feel good after you eat. I use spices, herbs, and acidity to build flavors and complexity into the dishes.

The chapters of this book are organized to reflect the distinct "seasons" of this semitropical growing region, as shaped by the ecology and climate. The hot, humid summers, long growing season, and short, cool, damp winters influence the way I cook and what I want to eat. "Oyster Season," when the southern waters are cold and crisp, allowing the shellfish to thrive, celebrates one of the defining mascots for the southeastern coast. Not only are oysters a significant food source, but their shells were used in the construction of the first homes built on the barrier islands and are still used to pave the roads today. "Vegetable Season," the most prominent growing season in this region, is a time of temperate climate and abundant produce. Carrots and sugar snap peas converge with cucumbers and the first signs of tomatoes. "Shrimp Season" pays respect to the industry that was once the economic stronghold of northeast Florida. This celebrated crustacean inspires yearly festivals and rivals the oyster in its symbolic importance in coastal cuisine. "Heat Season" is a title intended to highlight the brute force of the climate here. Summers are intense and make you slow down. Trees hang heavy, and humidity blankets the air. Only the most heat-resistant crops thrive in this season. The book ends its year-long adventure with "Smoke and Cedar Season," celebrating wood-fire cooking and the joy of being outdoors in the cool air.

There are times for indulging, and there are times for simplicity. This book is a set of recipes for all seasons of eating. Cooking is an adventure. Go light a fire, get outside, and look for that little bit of untamed Cumberland Island in your backyard, or wherever you may be.

A Guide to Good Cooking

SUCCESSFUL COOKING IS NOT just about having a good recipe. You also need a good workspace. It does not matter how small or how big your kitchen is; the key is to get comfortable in your space, be organized, and have fun. Your equipment and your ingredients will have a large impact on the results of your efforts. Below I have laid out some tips to help you navigate this book, source ingredients, and get the best equipment on your countertop.

Things to Remember When Making the Recipes in This Book

SALT

When I call for salt, I mean kosher salt. I recommend using Diamond Crystal kosher salt. When I call for sea salt specifically, use your favorite. I used Maldon sea salt for these recipes.

CONVECTION OVEN

All ovens are different. A convection oven has an interior fan that circulates the hot air, resulting in a quicker cook time. The recipes in this book were tested on a gas range with a convection oven. Keep that in mind when you cook and adjust the recipes as needed. If cooking in a non-convection oven, the dishes will need a little more time in the oven. Remember, use your instincts.

BUTTER

When I call for butter in this cookbook, use unsalted. When eating toast, use salted butter.

DAIRY

Any dairy in this cookbook is full fat. This includes milk, cream, buttermilk, and sour cream.

OIL

For frying, use neutral oils with high smoking points like canola or vegetable oil. For salad dressings, I like grapeseed oil for its neutral flavor. I like to keep two types of extra-virgin olive oil on hand, a milder and less expensive bottle for cooking and a specialty bottle, like *arbequina*, for finishing dishes. Unrefined coconut oil has a very specific flavor and is good for particular dishes like the delicious Grilled Coconut Chicken found on page 144. It solidifies when it is cold, so warm it up to get it back to its liquid state.

BREADCRUMBS

When I call for plain or unseasoned breadcrumbs in this cookbook, use store-bought panko. For an herbed breadcrumb recipe, see page 103.

CITRUS JUICE

When a recipe in this book calls for citrus juice, it's fresh squeezed.

FISH IN SEASON

Seafood is regional, and very often the varieties change depending on the season, so buy the best seafood you can find in your hometown—you can adjust these recipes to whatever fish you have on hand.

SHRIMP

Head-on shrimp are a sign of freshness. Even when the heads are frozen, they cannot last long, so if you are lucky enough to find head-on shrimp, use them immediately. If you are using shrimp tails, remember to adjust your recipe: 1 pound (455 g) head-on shrimp is equivalent to ½ pound (225 g) head-off shrimp.

Where to Buy Special Ingredients

If I can't find an ingredient from a brick-and-mortar purveyor, odds are I can easily find it online. The same is true for high-quality bakeware, knives, and small kitchenware. You can even find high-quality proteins such as wild shrimp online.

SPICES

Look for interesting spice shops close to where you live. For hard-to-find spices check out a few of my favorite sources that are available online:

- Le Sanctuaire in San Francisco
- SOS Chefs in New York City
- La Boîte in New York City

P.S. I love Aleppo pepper. This dried chile has a beautifully sweet and briny characteristic. It has a medium heat and is worthy of a place on your spice shelf.

CAROLINA GOLD RICE

Good-quality rice is a game changer. Go online to Anson Mills to buy Carolina Gold rice or look for producers in your area. Remember, different rices vary in cooking time, so adjust recipes to suit the type of rice you are using. Cornmeal, Sea Island red peas, and farro are just a handful of the amazing products that Anson Mills sells in addition to rice, so explore when you visit their site.

PRODUCE

Look for farmers' markets in your area for the freshest produce. Never underestimate produce that is locally grown—it has a huge impact on the flavor of your meal. No farmers' market available? Explore the produce section at your favorite grocery store. Request the fruits and vegetables you cannot find from the produce buyer in your market. For some of the unique, hard-to-find tropical fruits grown in Florida, check out MiamiFruit.org. They ship Florida-grown produce across the United States.

Building a Better Kitchen: Useful Equipment

Here are a few of my favorite tools to keep cooking easy. Build your kitchen piece by piece. These tools will last a long time.

- Blender: Vitamix
- Cast-iron pan: Lodge
- Chef knife: Check out the selection online at Korin, my favorite place to shop for a new knife
- Chinois (conical fine-mesh sieve)
- Deep-fry thermometer
- Dutch Oven: Le Creuset
- Heavy-bottom stainless-steel pots and pans: All-Clad, Analon
- Kitchen towels
- Measuring cups and spoons
- Meat thermometer: ThermoWorks
- Peeler: Kuhn Rikon
- Serrated knife: Messermeister
- Stainless-steel mixing bowls
- Stainless-steel spider strainer
- Tongs
- Very large wooden cutting board: Boos Blocks
- Whisk
- Zester: Microplane

A Guide to Building a Fire for Grilling

MANY OF THE RECIPES in this book are best when cooked over a fire and enjoyed outdoors. However, wherever possible, alternative instructions on how to make these recipes indoors, using your stovetop or oven, are provided in case you don't have access to a grill. If you are lucky enough to have access to an outdoor space, here is my guide to cooking over a fire.

TOOLS TO HAVE ON HAND

GRILL BRUSH

This is used to clean the grill grates. The best way is to heat the grate over the fire before brushing them; this will help to burn off any unwanted residue on the grates. Lightly oil the cleaned grates; this will help prevent food from sticking while grilling.

TONGS

A good set of metal tongs is the best tool for moving things around on the grill. Preferably ones that are about a foot (30.5 cm) in length, so your hands can stay a little farther away from the flames. I even use them to move around pieces of wood that are on fire when needed.

METAL SPATULA

This comes in handy when trying to flip over delicate items such as fish.

THICK KITCHEN TOWEL

I always like to have one handy in case I need to grab something that could be hot, such as a grill grate.

STEP 1 CHOOSE YOUR FUEL

FOR WOOD Use hardwoods such as hickory, oak, or pecan, as they produce a cleaner smoke and burn longer. Just make sure the wood is dry and has had time to age. Freshly fallen wood will be "green" and have too much moisture left in it. For grilling, I like to have the wood spilt into pieces no wider than 2 inches (5 cm). Wood left in large logs will take too long to burn down to coals. Kindling, small sticks or twigs that easily catch on fire, is important to have on hand.

FOR CHARCOAL I use natural lump wood charcoal, as it tends to be less processed than conventional briquettes and is the next best thing to using wood. If I don't have time to gather or chop wood for my grill, this is what I go for. That being said, if you prefer briquettes, by all means use those. You will still end up with more flavor than if you were using a gas grill.

STEP 2 BUILD YOUR FIRE

FOR WOOD Gather the amount of wood you think you will need for your fire—it's always better to have a little extra left over than not enough. In the center of your grill or fire pit, arrange some kindling—I use small thin strips of cedar, vertically stacked in the shape of a tepee. Next, stack smaller branches or strips of wood to build a log cabin–shaped formation around the kindling, making sure there are gaps to allow air into the fire. Build four or five layers up. Light the kindling and feed it to the fire as needed until the flames become established and the log cabin has caught on fire. Gradually begin to add more wood, building the fire to the size you will need to cook over. Be careful not to add too much at once and smother your fire. Airflow plays a key role.

FOR CHARCOAL I recommend using a chimney starter for charcoal. It's easy and efficient. Simply crumple up some newspaper or arrange a pile of kindling on the bottom of your grill or fire pit. Place the chimney starter on top of your newspaper or kindling. Pour the charcoal into the chimney starter and light the paper or kindling underneath it. The only downside to this is you can only fit so much charcoal into a chimney starter, so if you need a large fire you may want to have two chimney starters.

STEP 3 SPREAD THE COALS

FOR WOOD When using wood, you have to allow the fire enough time to transform the wood into beautiful glowing red coals; the time will vary depending on the size of the wood. When you have accumulated a good amount of coals, use a metal poker or branch of wood to spread the coals around the grill. Gauge your fire. If you think you will need more heat, this is a good time to add more wood. Place your grill grate over the fire to heat up before cooking.

FOR CHARCOAL If using the chimney starter, it's pretty easy: Grab the handle and carefully pour the coals out into your grill. The coals should be glowing red with flames when you dump them out. Place your grill grate over the coals to heat up before cooking.

STEP 4 KNOW THE TEMPERATURE OF THE COALS

Depending on what you are grilling, you will want to have your fire at different temperatures. For some items you want a hot, intense heat to quickly sear the item without it overcooking. Other items need lower heat to allow even cooking to a desired doneness without becoming scorched on the outside. The tips offered below apply to both wood fires and charcoal fires.

HIGH HEAT The coals are bright red and orange, and small flames are still burning. I use this temperature for items like the grilled oysters (page 68) and grilled lettuce (page 237).

MEDIUM HEAT The coals are glowing red, and have an occasional flame pop up. This is the temperature I use the most. Check out the recipes for zucchini escabeche (page 158) or whole grilled fish (page 275).

LOW HEAT The coals are mostly white with ash and have a touch of glowing red with no flames. I use this temperature for items such as Grilled Coconut Chicken (page 144) and the Banana Leaf–Wrapped Snapper (page 264).

Recipe for Writing a Cookbook

DURING THE PROCESS OF MAKING this book, I took a trip to Cuba, where I learned that strong, sweet espresso is essential to daily life. You wake up, you drink coffee. You walk to a plaza, then sit and drink coffee. You visit friends, they offer you coffee. I took this lesson home with me. When it comes time to take years' worth of kitchen notes and turn them into a book, drink copious amount of sweet, Cuban-style coffee. I make this with a 3-cup (720 ml) Bialetti moka pot, which is perfect for two people.

Cuban-Style Coffee

MAKES 2 ESPRESSO-SIZE SERVINGS

2	TABLESPOONS FINELY GROUND COFFEE
1½	TABLESPOONS SUGAR
⅓	CUP (75 ML) OAT MILK (SEE NOTE)

Pour ¾ cup (180 ml) water into the bottom half of a moka pot, making sure to keep the water level just below the steam vent. Insert the metal portafilter and add the ground coffee. Screw the moka pot together tightly. Heat the moka pot over medium-low heat with the lid open. Put the sugar in a small cup. While the coffee is heating, put the oat milk in a small pot and bring to a simmer, whisking to froth.

When the first bit of coffee begins to brew, take 1 tablespoon and add it to the sugar. Close the lid and return the pot to the stovetop to finish brewing and remove from the heat when done. Use a spoon to beat the sugar and coffee into a light *espuma*. (This will form a frothy top to your coffee, similar to the crema found on espresso.) Pour the coffee over the *espuma* and gently stir. Divide the coffee between two cups and top with the lightly frothed oat milk.

NOTE *I use oat milk when I make this but feel free to substitute regular cow's milk.*

PULL ON YOUR MUD BOOTS and grab your oyster knife. These are the cool, gray days of winter. Oysters and clams are at their peak, sitting plump and sweet in the cold Atlantic water while bitter greens grow abundant and tart-bright citrus sits ripe and heavy on the island's trees. Stacks of cedar and oak are burned down on crisp winter nights for cooking the season's best seafood, and shared with gratitude in a season to indulge. Nor'easters blow the damp, cold air, and the empty beaches are littered with shells washed ashore from distant storms.

This is a time to eat in decadence. Fresh oysters and clams are cooked in a fennel-spiked chowder, slow-roasted root vegetables are gently caramelized in the heat of the oven, and buttermilk-brined pork chops are fried to crispy, golden perfection in a cast-iron pan. These favored recipes create a respite from the cold winter months.

OYSTER

SEASON

Blood Orange and Ginger Soda

MAKES 1
(11-OUNCE/
330 ML) DRINK

WHEN YOU START TO DRINK fresh-squeezed citrus juice, it is hard to go back to store bought. Traveling through Spain, I was amazed by the amount of fresh-squeezed citrus readily available. Every little bar or café that I would swing by had perfect little orange-juicing machines. I carried this learned lesson home with me. Come citrus season in the kitchen, we take full advantage of the bounty. While making various dishes, we sometimes leave behind citrus "bones" that beg to be juiced. Cara Cara, Minneloa, blood orange, grapefruit—this recipe has endless variations depending on what you have on hand. The fresh ginger offers a perfect little kick.

2   TABLESPOONS HONEY GINGER SYRUP (recipe follows)

½   CUP (120 ML) CARA CARA ORANGE JUICE, strained

¼   CUP (60 ML) BLOOD ORANGE JUICE, strained

4   OUNCES (120 ML) COLD SODA WATER

    ICE (optional)

Mix the ginger syrup and Cara Cara and blood orange juices in a glass. Top with soda water and gently stir. Add the ice if you like.

Honey Ginger Syrup MAKES 1 CUP (240 ML)

1½   TABLESPOONS HONEY

1   (1-INCH/2.5 CM) PIECE FRESH GINGER, peeled and finely grated

In a small pot, combine 1 cup (240 ml) water, the honey, and ginger. Cook over high heat until the syrup reaches a boil. Remove from the heat and let steep for 5 minutes. Strain the syrup through a fine-mesh sieve into a bowl and discard the solids. Let cool completely before using. Store in the refrigerator for up to 2 weeks.

SEVERAL TIMES A YEAR I go on an oatmeal kick. It's a breakfast that is healthy and hearty enough to keep me going through a busy day in the kitchen. I have grown especially fond of topping it with a pat of butter and then dousing it with cinnamon milk until it becomes slightly soupy. A handful of crunchy seeds and nuts make a nice addition.

Cold-Weather Breakfast of Steel-Cut Oats

with Jammy Blackberries and Cinnamon Milk

SERVES 2

- 1 CUP (120 ML) ALMOND MILK
- 1 CUP (155 G) STEEL-CUT OATS (see Note)
- 1 TABLESPOON BROWN SUGAR
- 1 TABLESPOON HONEY
- ¼ TEASPOON SALT
- ½ CUP (120 ML) CINNAMON MILK (recipe follows)
- ½ CUP (120 ML) JAMMY BLACKBERRIES (recipe follows)
- 2 TABLESPOONS CHOPPED AND TOASTED PECANS
- 1 TABLESPOON CHOPPED AND TOASTED PUMPKIN SEEDS
- 1 TABLESPOON TOASTED BENNE SEEDS

In a medium pot, combine 2 cups water, the almond milk, oats, brown sugar, honey, and salt. Bring to a gentle simmer over medium heat, stirring occasionally. Reduce the heat to medium-low and cook, stirring often, until the oats are tender and the mixture has thickened, about 20 minutes. Remove from the heat. Ladle into bowls and top with the cinnamon milk and blackberries. Divide the toasted pecans, pumpkin seeds, and benne seeds between each bowl.

NOTE *Check the label and adjust the ratio of oats to cooking liquid if needed. Not all oats are the same.*

Cinnamon Milk MAKES ½ CUP (120 ML)

- ½ CUP (120 ML) ALMOND MILK
- 1½ TEASPOONS BROWN SUGAR
- ¼ TEASPOON GROUND CINNAMON

In a small pot over medium-low heat, combine all of the ingredients. Bring to a simmer. Whisk well to incorporate the cinnamon. Remove from the heat and serve with the oatmeal. You can serve it on top or on the side, hot or cold. Serve it the way you like it.

Jammy Blackberries MAKES ½ CUP (120 ML)

- 6 OUNCES (170 G) FRESH BLACKBERRIES
- 1½ TABLESPOONS BROWN SUGAR
- 1 TABLESPOON LEMON JUICE

In a small pot over medium heat, combine all of the ingredients. Cook, stirring often, until thickened and the blackberries begin to break down, about 12 minutes. Serve warm on top of or alongside the oatmeal.

Radicchio Flatbread

with Ricotta and Chile Oil

MAKES 2 (8-INCH/20 CM) FLATBREADS

I LOVE BITTER GREENS, but it's a relationship I learned how to navigate. If you set a big plate of radicchio, rapini, or dandelion greens in front of someone without the right preparation, odds are you will make an enemy, converting them into lifelong haters of these glorious veggies. There are two ingredients that can be used to soften the bitter blow: acid and fat. When serving as a salad, toss with an acidic vinaigrette. The acid helps to balance the bitter flavors. When cooking, sauté the greens with fresh lemon juice and some olive oil or butter. The more acid you add, the less bitter the greens become, and the fat helps to round out all of these flavors. This flatbread topping has lemon juice to mellow the bitter notes, and lush ricotta for richness.

1	SMALL HEAD OF RADICCHIO
2	TABLESPOONS LEMON JUICE
½	TEASPOON KOSHER SALT
2	(5½-OUNCE/155 G) PORTIONS FLATBREAD DOUGH *(recipe follows)*
	ALL-PURPOSE FLOUR, *as needed for dusting*
2	TABLESPOONS OLIVE OIL
8	OUNCES (225 G) RICOTTA
2	TEASPOONS CHILE FLAKES
2	TEASPOONS CHOPPED FRESH PARSLEY
1	TEASPOON SEA SALT
2	TABLESPOONS CHILE OIL *(recipe follows)*

Flatbread Dough

MAKES 4 (5½-OUNCE/155 G) PORTIONS

¾	CUP (180 ML) WARM WATER
1	TEASPOON HONEY
¼	OUNCE (7 G) ACTIVE DRY YEAST
2	CUPS (255 G) ALL-PURPOSE FLOUR, *plus extra for dusting*
½	CUP (120 ML) PLAIN GREEK YOGURT
2	TABLESPOONS OLIVE OIL, *plus extra for the bowl*
½	TEASPOON SALT
½	TEASPOON SMOKED PAPRIKA

Preheat the oven to 400°F (205°C).

Cut the radicchio into wedges, separate the leaves, wash, and dry. Toss with the lemon juice and kosher salt and set aside.

On a well-floured surface, roll out one portion of dough into an 8-inch (20 cm) round, about ¼ inch (6 mm) thick. Use flour liberally on the table and rolling pin so the dough will not stick.

In a large cast-iron pan, heat 1 tablespoon of the olive oil over medium-high heat. When the oil is hot, gently place the dough round flat in the pan. Cook for 1 to 2 minutes, or until the dough begins to gently brown and bubbles begin appearing. Flip the dough and cook for 1 minute. Transfer the flatbread to a baking sheet lined with parchment. Repeat the process for the second portion of dough.

Top each flatbread with half of the ricotta, radicchio, chile flakes, parsley, and sea salt.

Place the sheet pan in the oven and bake for 10 minutes. Remove from the oven and drizzle each flatbread with 1 tablespoon of the chile oil. Eat immediately.

In a bowl, mix the water, honey, and yeast. Place in a warm spot for 10 minutes to allow the yeast to bloom. Add the flour, yogurt, oil, salt, and smoked paprika. Mix to form a ball.

Generously dust a countertop with flour. Knead the dough for 5 minutes on the counter. Use flour on your hands and the counter as needed; the dough should never stick to the counter.

Place the kneaded dough in a lightly oiled bowl and cover. Set aside to rest for 1 hour at room temperature. The dough will double in volume.

Divide the dough into four 5½-ounce (155 g) portions. Any dough that you are not using can be tightly wrapped in plastic wrap and frozen for up to 1 month.

Chile Oil MAKES ½ CUP (120 ML)

¼ CUP (60 ML) OLIVE OIL

¼ CUP (60 ML) CANOLA OIL
   OR OTHER NEUTRAL OIL

2 TEASPOONS SMOKED PAPRIKA

¼ TEASPOON CAYENNE POWDER

¼ TEASPOON SALT

1 BAY LEAF

1 SPRIG OF THYME

1 SPRIG OF ROSEMARY

1 CLOVE GARLIC, *peeled*

Combine all of the ingredients in a small pot. Warm over medium heat. Just as the garlic begins to lightly simmer, remove from the heat and let the oil sit for 10 minutes. Pour through a fine-mesh strainer into a bowl and reserve the oil; discard the solids. The oil can be stored at room temperature for up to 3 months.

THE SECRET'S IN THE STOCK. This stands true for any soup, but especially this one. Ham hocks are deeply flavorful cuts of meat that are great for building flavor. They produce a gelatinous broth that enriches any vegetable that it is cooked with, ham hocks being the secret weapon of southern classics such as collard greens and long-braised green beans. The bitter note of the turnip green pistou balances the rich meaty broth. Purchase ham hocks that have been cured and smoked for a complex flavor. They consist of mostly bone, so they need to be simmered long and carefully picked to extract the meat. Preparing them is truly a labor of love. Look online for one of the many famous southern smokehouses, likes Benton's or Newsom's, to find the best ham hocks (and pick up a little country ham while you're at it).

Winter Root Vegetable Soup

with
Ham Hock
and Turnip
Green Pistou

MAKES 8 CUPS
(2 L); SERVES
4 TO 6

1	(1½-POUND/680 G) SMOKED HAM HOCK
1½	ONIONS, *diced small*
2	TABLESPOONS OLIVE OIL
3	SMALL LEEKS, *diced small (about 1½ cups/150 g)*
2	CLOVES GARLIC, *minced*
¾	CUP (180 ML) WHITE WINE
1	RUTABAGA, *diced small (about 1½ cups/200 g)*
2	MEDIUM TURNIPS, *diced small (about 1½ cups/200 g)*
3	CARROTS, *diced small (about 1½ cups/200 g)*
¼	TEASPOON FRESHLY GROUND BLACK PEPPER
4	CUPS (960 ML) CHICKEN STOCK
2	BAY LEAVES
1	TABLESPOON SALT
2	TABLESPOONS CHOPPED FRESH PARSLEY
1	CUP (240 ML) TURNIP GREEN PISTOU *(recipe follows)*
½	CUP (50 G) FRESHLY GRATED PARMESAN CHEESE
	CRUSTY BREAD

Put the ham hock in a medium pot and cover with water. Bring to a boil. Remove from the heat and drain off the liquid. This will help rinse away some of the excess salt from curing.

Put the ham hock back in the pot, cover with 8 cups (2 L) water, and add half of the diced onions. Bring to a boil, then reduce the heat to a simmer. Cook until the meat is tender and easily pulls away from the bone, about 50 minutes. Remove the ham hock from the cooking liquid, strain the liquid, and reserve

2½ cups (600 ml) of the ham stock for the soup. Pick the meat from the ham hock, and roughly chop it; this should yield about 1 cup (200 g) chopped meat.

In a large pot, heat the oil over medium heat. Add the remaining diced onions, the leeks, and garlic. Cook for 3 minutes, stirring frequently. Add the wine. Reduce for 1 minute. Add the rutabaga, turnips, carrots, and pepper. Cook for 3 minutes. Add the chopped ham hock meat, the reserved ham stock, the chicken stock, and bay leaves. Bring to a simmer and cook for 15 minutes, or until the vegetables are tender. Stir in the salt and parsley.

To serve, ladle the soup into bowls and top with pistou, a little cheese, and a hunk of bread.

Turnip Green Pistou MAKES 1 CUP (240 ML)

¾	CUP (180 ML) OLIVE OIL
1½	TABLESPOONS LEMON JUICE
	ZEST OF ½ LEMON
1	CLOVE GARLIC
4	OUNCES (115 G) TURNIP GREENS, *cleaned and chopped*
¼	CUP (25 G) FINELY GRATED PARMESAN CHEESE
½	TEASPOON SALT

Put all the ingredients in a blender and pulse until smooth.

Oyster and Clam Chowder

SERVES 4

I CRAVE CHOWDER ON cold winter days on the coast. I like to use the weather as an excuse to eat with indulgence, and chowders with cream-laden broth spiked with briny shellfish and tart lemon top my list of all-time comfort foods. I like to use both clams and oysters in my chowder, paying tribute to the popular oyster stews of the Southeast.

¼ CUP (55 G) BUTTER

2 SHALLOTS, *minced*

3 RIBS CELERY, *diced small (about 1 cup/100 g)*

1 FENNEL BULB, *diced small (about 1 cup/100 g)*

2 SMALL LEEKS, *diced small (about 1 cup/100 g)*

3 CLOVES GARLIC, *minced*

2 CUPS (280 G) PEELED AND SMALL-DICE RED POTATOES

½ CUP (120 ML) WHITE WINE

1 BAY LEAF

2½ CUPS (600 ML) CLAM JUICE, *reserved from steaming clams and extra as needed (see Note)*

30 STEAMED CLAMS *(recipe follows)*

16 OYSTERS, *shucked*

1 CUP (240 ML) HEAVY CREAM

ZEST OF ½ LEMON

3 DASHES OF TABASCO SAUCE

½ TEASPOON SALT

1 TEASPOON THINLY SLICED FRESH CHIVES

1 TEASPOON CHOPPED FRESH PARSLEY

1 TEASPOON CHILE FLAKES

SALTINE CRACKERS *(because chowder is better with saltines)*

In a large pot over medium-low heat, melt the butter. Add the shallots, celery, fennel, leeks, garlic, and potatoes. Cook for 10 minutes, stirring frequently. Add the wine. Reduce for 2 minutes. Add the bay leaf and clam juice. Bring to a simmer and cook until the potatoes are tender, about 10 minutes. Add the chopped clams, oysters, cream, lemon zest, and Tabasco sauce. Simmer for 1 minute. Taste for seasoning, as clams will have varying degrees of salinity.

Ladle into bowls and top with chives, parsley, and a pinch of chile flakes. Serve with the saltines.

NOTE *Your steamed clams will not yield enough liquid. Plan to have at least 1½ cups (360 ml) bottled clam juice on hand.*

Steamed Clams MAKES ABOUT 30 CLAMS

½ CUP (120 ML) WHITE WINE

2½ POUNDS (1.2 KG) LITTLENECK CLAMS (about 30)

In a medium pot over medium-high heat, combine the wine and ½ cup (120 ml) water and bring to a simmer. Add the clams and cover the pot. Steam for 5 minutes. Remove the lid and pick out any opened clams. If any clams remain closed, cover and continue to steam, regularly checking and removing any opened clams until all have been steamed. Discard any that refuse to open. Strain the cooking liquid and set aside for chowder.

When the clams are cool to the touch, remove the meat and discard the shells. Roughly chop the meat and set aside for chowder.

WARNING: IF YOU LEAVE your plate of fried oysters unattended, they will never make it to the salad. This recipe yields perfectly crunchy oysters that are good enough to eat alone. Convert your non-oyster-eating friends with a bowl of these. The southeast coast is famed for its fish camps, rustic seafood restaurants that serve up the local catch. No establishment would open its doors without fried oysters on the menu. Layering it on a salad is a perfect way to add balance to the indulgence of eating fried seafood. Peppery radish, tart buttermilk dressing, and fresh herbs make this a bright addition to a winter menu.

Fried Oyster Salad

with
Radish and
Buttermilk
Dressing

SERVES 4

6	OUNCES (170 G) LOOSE-LEAF LETTUCES
2	OR 3 WINTER RADISHES, *cut in half and thinly sliced into half-moons*
½	TEASPOON SEA SALT
	PINCH OF FRESHLY GROUND BLACK PEPPER
1	TEASPOON LEMON JUICE
1	TABLESPOON OLIVE OIL
1	CUP (240 ML) BUTTERMILK DRESSING *(recipe follows)*
1	TABLESPOON CHOPPED FRESH PARSLEY
1	TABLESPOON CHOPPED FRESH CHERVIL
20	FRIED OYSTERS *(recipe follows)*

In a mixing bowl, put the lettuces, radish, salt, pepper, lemon juice, and olive oil. Gently toss to combine and transfer to a serving platter. Drizzle ½ cup (120 ml) of the dressing over the salad. Add the parsley and chervil and top with the fried oysters. Serve immediately.

Serve with the remaining ½ cup (120 ml) dressing on the side for people to use as they like.

Buttermilk Dressing MAKES 1½ CUPS (360 ML)

½	SMALL SHALLOT, *finely minced*
	ZEST OF 1 LEMON
2	TABLESPOONS LEMON JUICE
1½	TEASPOONS MINCED FRESH PARSLEY
¾	TEASPOON SALT
¼	TEASPOON FRESHLY GROUND BLACK PEPPER
½	CUP (120 ML) SOUR CREAM
¼	CUP (60 ML) MAYONNAISE
¾	CUP (180 ML) BUTTERMILK

In a bowl, mix together all of the ingredients. Refrigerate, for up to 5 days, until ready to use.

Fried Oysters MAKES 20 OYSTERS

4	CUPS (960 ML) CANOLA OIL
1	CUP (240 ML) BUTTERMILK
1	TABLESPOON TABASCO SAUCE
1	TABLESPOON SALT
1	TEASPOON GARLIC POWDER
1	TEASPOON ONION POWDER
1	TEASPOON PAPRIKA
½	CUP (70 G) FINE YELLOW CORNMEAL
½	CUP (65 G) ALL-PURPOSE FLOUR
1	CUP (100 G) FINE BREADCRUMBS
20	OYSTERS, *shucked*

In a medium pot, heat the oil to 350°F (175°C).

In a bowl, whisk together the buttermilk and Tabasco sauce. In a separate bowl, whisk together the salt, garlic powder, onion powder, paprika, cornmeal, flour, and breadcrumbs. Add the shucked oysters to the buttermilk mixture to coat. Remove the oysters from the buttermilk and place them in the cornmeal dredge. Toss to coat them evenly and transfer to a wire rack until ready to fry.

Working in batches, gently lower the oysters into the oil and fry until golden brown and crispy, about 2½ minutes. Remove them with a slotted spoon and set aside on a paper towel–lined plate to cool slightly.

A Note on
CITRUS

Popular culture solidified citrus as an icon of Florida's landscape. Oranges adorn the license plates. Gas station billboards beckon travelers with signs endorsing fresh-squeezed juice and green mesh bags of freshly picked citrus. Oranges still dominate the state's agricultural production, with grapefruits and limes close behind. The abundance of these sweet and acidic fruits have worked their way into the regional cuisine, blending beautifully with the Caribbean influence that enriches the fabric of southern cooking.

In this landscape, citrus trees are everywhere. Citrus season is eagerly anticipated all year, as we watch the fragrant orange blossoms bloom in spring and the small fruit begin to grow through the summer. By fall, lime-green ornaments are visible in the branches. Harvest can begin as early as November, but the height of citrus season in Florida is February.

Citrus season is my winter salvation. As the colder months roll around, food inevitably takes on richer flavors. Cream-based chowders and rich braised meats are a necessity for keeping warm. Citrus sweeps in, brightening menus and balancing flavors. On Cumberland, we gather citrus from the trees that grow near the inn. Two bitter orange trees adorn my little cottage, while a short walk down to the garden gives us access to lip-puckering calamondin. Walking the same distance in the opposite direction we find tartly sweet grapefruit. In the kitchen, we preserve calamondin in salt, juice grapefruit for tarts, and braise pork in orange and island bay.

Lemons, limes, oranges, and grapefruit can be found year round in the grocery store, but look closer. In the winter, all of the citrus is just a little plumper and a little juicier with hard-to-find varieties more widely available. Look for blood oranges with their deep red flesh and slightly sour flavor. Satsumas are a variety of mandarin orange that are considerably more juicy. Cara Cara is a variety of orange with a blush pink interior, sweet flavor, and low acidity. It is worth experimenting with these less typical varieties, which tend to offer more complex flavors in comparison to the mainstream options.

Winter Citrus Salad

with Feta, Pumpkin Seeds, and Beldi Olive Vinaigrette

SERVES 2

THE TRICK TO A good salad is the balance of textures. Personally, I need crunch. Finding the right crunch for a salad is a creative endeavor. Croutons, a classic. Nuts and seeds, endless options there. Fried quinoa, delicious and unexpected. Crumbled crackers, so good. Sometimes the lettuces can supply the crunch. A romaine heart can stand up to a lot of toppings and retain its crisp texture. Maybe that's why it's so popular? During the cold winter months, sweet citrus is at its peak and is the only fruit that grows on Cumberland Island. For this homage to the fruit of winter, pumpkin seeds add the crunch, feta is pleasantly briny and rich, and olives add the umami.

½ SMALL HEAD OF RADICCHIO

1 CARA CARA ORANGE OR BLOOD ORANGE, *or a mix of the two*

2 BIG HANDFULS OF LOOSE-LEAF LETTUCES

¼ CUP (40 G) CRUMBLED FETA CHEESE

2 TABLESPOONS SPICED PUMPKIN SEEDS *(recipe follows)*

2 TABLESPOONS OLIVE VINAIGRETTE *(recipe follows)*

PINCH OF SEA SALT

Cut the radicchio into wedges and separate the leaves. Remove the peel and pith of the orange. Cut in half and then cut into half-moon slices.

Toss the radicchio leaves and loose-leaf lettuces together in a bowl. Place the lettuces on a plate and top with the slices of citrus, the feta crumbles, and pumpkin seeds. Drizzle with the vinaigrette and add a pinch of salt. Serve immediately.

Spiced Pumpkin Seeds MAKES 1 CUP (120 G)

1 CUP (65 G) HULLED PUMPKIN SEEDS OR PEPITAS

1 TEASPOON OLIVE OIL

½ TEASPOON SALT

1 TEASPOON GROUND CORIANDER

½ TEASPOON GROUND CUMIN

Preheat the oven to 325°F (165°C).

In a bowl, toss the pumpkin seeds, oil, salt, coriander, and cumin together. Spread on a baking sheet. Bake until very fragrant and a light golden color, about 6 minutes. Cool to room temperature. They can be stored for up to 1 month in an airtight container.

Beldi Olive Vinaigrette MAKES 2 CUPS (480 ML)

¼ CUP (60 ML) LEMON JUICE

¼ CUP (60 ML) CHAMPAGNE VINEGAR

½ TEASPOON SALT

¾ CUP (180 ML) OLIVE OIL

½ CUP (120 ML) GRAPESEED OIL

1 TABLESPOON ZA'ATAR SPICE BLEND

¼ CUP (40 G) PITTED AND CHOPPED BELDI OLIVES *(see Note)*

1 TEASPOON CHOPPED FRESH PARSLEY

In a bowl, mix the lemon juice, vinegar, and salt. Slowly whisk in the olive oil and grapeseed oil. Add the za'atar, olives, and parsley and whisk together. Store in the refrigerator for up to 2 weeks. Set out at room temperature for 15 minutes before serving.

NOTE *Beldi olives are oil-cured olives from Morocco that have a deep, fruity flavor and meaty texture. If unavailable near you, just substitute your favorite olives.*

GIVE ME POTATO CHIPS and French fries any day. I love crispy potatoes in all forms. When serving potatoes as a side dish, I find it incredibly appropriate to make them such an irresistibly crunchy delight that you can't put them down. Covered with Parmesan cheese, lemon zest, and herbs, these potatoes are an indulgence. Add a generous helping of pungent horseradish cream for the finishing touch.

Crispy Smashed Potatoes

with Horseradish and Sea Salt

SERVES 4

1   POUND (455 G) FINGERLING OR BABY POTATOES

2   TABLESPOONS KOSHER SALT

¼   CUP (60 ML) CANOLA OIL

1   TABLESPOON BUTTER

3   TABLESPOONS FINELY GRATED PARMESAN CHEESE

1   TABLESPOON CHOPPED FRESH PARSLEY

1   TABLESPOON THINLY SLICED FRESH CHIVES

1   TEASPOON FINELY GRATED LEMON ZEST

1   TEASPOON SMOKED PAPRIKA

¼   TEASPOON FRESHLY GROUND BLACK PEPPER

1   TEASPOON SEA SALT

½   CUP (120 ML) HORSERADISH CREAM *(recipe follows)*

In a medium pot, combine the potatoes, kosher salt, and 4 cups (960 ml) water. Bring to a boil over high heat. Reduce the heat to a gentle simmer and cook for 12 minutes, or until the potatoes are cooked through but still firm. Drain the potatoes and put them in the refrigerator to cool.

Cut the potatoes into 1-inch (2.5 cm), bite-size pieces. Using the palm of your hand, gently press the potatoes to flatten them.

In a large cast-iron pan, heat the oil over medium-high heat until very hot. Add the potatoes and arrange them in a single layer. Cook until golden brown, about 5 minutes. Flip them over and continue to cook for another 5 minutes, occasionally shaking the pan. You are looking for an even golden-brown color on both sides.

Pour off the excess oil from the pan and add the butter to the pan. When the butter is melted, remove the pan from the heat. Add the cheese, parsley, chives, lemon zest, smoked paprika, and pepper and toss to coat the potatoes in the still-warm pan so that the cheese starts to melt. Sprinkle the potatoes with the sea salt. Serve immediately with a big fat wallop of horseradish cream.

Horseradish Cream MAKES ½ CUP (120 ML)

¼   CUP (60 ML) SOUR CREAM

2   TABLESPOONS MAYONNAISE

2   TABLESPOONS GRATED HORSERADISH, *fresh or prepared*

1   TEASPOON WORCESTERSHIRE SAUCE

¼   TEASPOON TABASCO SAUCE

¼   TEASPOON SALT

    PINCH OF FRESHLY GROUND BLACK PEPPER

In a bowl, whisk all of the ingredients together. Store in the refrigerator for up to 5 days.

Simple Roasted Carrots

SERVES 4

THERE IS AN UNSPOKEN TRUTH to using the word *simple* in a recipe. Yes, it implies ease of preparation and production. But simple recipes will unapologetically reveal the quality of your ingredients. The better your carrot, the better this dish will taste. Sweet carrots, hand harvested from cold soil, tossed with fresh herbs and honey, are a perfect winter side dish. Look for heirloom varieties like Mokum and Thumbelina at your local farmers' markets. Rainbow carrots are more and more common in the grocery store. Carrots with their tops still attached are a good sign of freshness. An added bonus to this dish is the whole roasted garlic. Squeeze out the caramelized garlic bits from the bulb for added depth and satisfaction.

1½	POUNDS (680 G) BABY CARROTS, *cleaned and topped*
1	TABLESPOON OLIVE OIL
2	TEASPOONS HONEY
1	TEASPOON SALT
¼	TEASPOON GROUND CORIANDER
¼	TEASPOON GROUND CUMIN
3	MEDIUM SHALLOTS, *peeled and cut into quarters*
1	WHOLE HEAD OF GARLIC, *cut in half horizontally*
5	SPRIGS ROSEMARY
3	SPRIGS THYME

Preheat the oven to 375°F (190°C).

In a bowl, put the carrots, olive oil, honey, salt, coriander, and cumin and toss to coat the carrots evenly. Add in the shallots and garlic and toss. Spread on a baking sheet in a single layer. Top with the rosemary and thyme sprigs. Roast until the carrots are tender and caramelized, 20 to 25 minutes. Serve immediately.

WHEN MY SISTER COMES to visit from California, her number-one meal request is fried pork chops with gravy. Neither my sister nor I grew up cooking or eating pork, so this dish was a revelation. Ben grew up in Georgia, learning classic southern cooking from his grandmother, and this recipe is a reflection of the time they spent together in the kitchen. Thinly pounded pork loin dredged in flour and fried in a cast-iron pan, then smothered with sawmill gravy— it's a decadent treat. We spike the gravy with wild bay laurel that grows abundantly along the coast, but this recipe assumes you'll be using dried bay leaves, which will have the same effect. To complete the meal, we usually cook up some field peas (page 197) and buttermilk biscuits (page 183).

Fried Pork Chops

and Bay Laurel Gravy

SERVES 4

4	(4-OUNCE/115 G) PORTIONS OF PORK LOIN, *trimmed of excess fat*
1	CUP (240 ML) BUTTERMILK
1	TABLESPOON TABASCO SAUCE
1	CUP (125 G) ALL-PURPOSE FLOUR
¾	TEASPOON GARLIC POWDER
¾	TEASPOON ONION POWDER
1	TEASPOON FRESHLY GROUND BLACK PEPPER
1½	TEASPOONS SALT
½	TEASPOON CAYENNE POWDER
½	TEASPOON PAPRIKA
½	TEASPOON GROUND FENNEL SEEDS
1¼	CUPS (300 ML) CANOLA OIL
2	CUPS (450 ML) BAY LAUREL GRAVY *(recipe follows)*

Place the pork loin on a cutting board and cover with plastic wrap. Flatten to ½ inch (12 mm) thick by hitting with a meat mallet or small cast-iron pan. Put in a bowl and cover with the buttermilk and Tabasco. Marinate for 30 minutes.

While the pork chops marinate, make the dredge: In a bowl, whisk together the flour, garlic powder, onion powder, black pepper, salt, cayenne, paprika, and fennel. Set aside 5 table-spoons of the dredge for the gravy.

Remove the pork from the buttermilk mixture, shaking off any excess. Coat each side in the seasoned flour. Place on a wire rack.

In a 12-inch (30.5 cm) cast-iron pan, heat the oil to 350°F (177°C) over medium heat. You can test the oil by adding a pinch of flour—it will sizzle and float right away. Fry two pork chops at a time. The oil should reach to halfway up the sides of the pork chops. Press down in the middle of the chops to ensure even browning. Cook for about 4 minutes on the first side. When the pork chops are golden brown, flip over and cook for 3 minutes. Remove from the oil and place the pork chops on a plate lined with a paper towel. Repeat the process for the two remaining pork chops. Reserve 5 tablespoons (75 ml) of the used frying oil for the gravy, discarding the rest. Serve the pork chops on a large platter with the gravy on the side. Trust me, make the gravy!

Bay Laurel Gravy MAKES 2 CUPS (480 ML)

5	TABLESPOONS (75 ML) RESERVED FRYING OIL
5	TABLESPOONS (35 G) RESERVED DREDGE
3	BAY LEAVES
2	CUPS (480 ML) MILK
1	TEASPOON SALT
	PINCH OF FRESHLY GROUND BLACK PEPPER
3	DASHES OF TABASCO SAUCE

In the same 12-inch (30.5 cm) cast-iron pan that you cooked the pork chops, heat the reserved frying oil over medium heat. When oil is hot, add the reserved dredge. Cook for 2 minutes, stirring constantly. Add the bay leaves and ½ cup (120 ml) of the milk. Whisk to smooth any lumps. As the gravy thickens, continue to add the milk in ½-cup (120 ml) increments, continuing to whisk. When the gravy reaches a boil, remove from the heat and season with salt, pepper, and Tabasco sauce. Serve immediately.

Marsh Mud and Sea Salt:

THE SOUTHEAST'S WILD OYSTER

Grassy and full of salinity, sweet and balanced, buttery notes, meaty and clean. These are just a few of the flavors of the incredible oysters that are growing in the Southeast. In recent years, the number of oysters coming from this region has increased dramatically as the southern states have embraced aquaculture. But there is one stalwart in the crowd: the rare wild Georgia oyster.

No outside seed varieties are allowed to grow along the hundred-mile stretch of Georgia coast. All of the oysters must be grown from wild seed that is currently being propagated by the University of Georgia marine extension program. Limited licenses are available to harvest these beauties, which means fewer Georgia oyster are available to the public.

The regulations of the Georgia coast also impact the appearance of these wild oysters. The "singles," the individual cupped oysters favored by restaurants serving mile-high shellfish platters, are not a true picture of the wild oysters that grow on the oyster reefs in the intracoastal waterway. Razor-sharp oyster mounds grow in clusters, piling high in the marsh mud. Described best as the country cousins of singles, these oysters are labor intensive to harvest, need a good scrubbing to remove the marsh mud, and require a skilled hand to shuck. But the rewards are generous. Grown in clean, remote waters, they have a high salinity and a crisp, sweet flavor with a touch of lemongrass—a characteristic of the cordgrass that also gives Georgia shrimp their distinct sweet note.

If you are lucky enough to see Harris Neck or Cumberland oysters on a menu, order a dozen.

Wood-Fired Oysters

with Hot Sauce
Butter
and
Breadcrumbs

SERVES 4; MAKES
48 OYSTERS

THESE OYSTERS HAVE AN EFFECT on people. One minute you're standing around chatting, enjoying good conversation and a shared evening. The next, silent competitive eating—nothing but the slurping of fat, little oysters that are drowned and charred in a slightly spicy, buttery pool, followed by the clacking of the empty shells hitting the plate. If it's too cold to go outside and grill, throw these delicious oysters on a makeshift grill in your fireplace. Don't have a fireplace? Roast them in the oven. Just find a way to make these oysters.

1	CUP (2 STICKS/225 G) BUTTER, *at room temperature*
2	TABLESPOONS CHOLULA HOT SAUCE OR A SIMILAR BRAND
1	CLOVE GARLIC, *minced*
¼	TEASPOON SALT
4	DOZEN SMALL OYSTERS, *about 2 inches (5 cm) long*
1	CUP (75 G) HERBED BREADCRUMBS *(page 103)*

In a bowl, mix the butter, hot sauce, minced garlic, and salt. Stir together until smooth and well combined.

Build a fire in a grill and let it burn down to high heat (see Note).

While the fire is burning down, shuck the oysters, reserving the meat and liquid in the bottom half of each shell.

Top each oyster with a dollop of hot sauce butter and a healthy pinch of breadcrumbs. Place them on the grill and cook until the butter melts and bubbles and begins to brown on the edges, 3 to 5 minutes. Serve immediately.

NOTE *If you can't cook the oysters on a grill, use your oven. Preheat the oven to 425°F (220°C). Place the oysters on a baking sheet and cook until the butter melts and bubbles and begins to brown on the edges, 3 to 5 minutes. Serve immediately.*

Fisherman's-Style Local Catch

SERVES 4 TO 6

A FAVORED LOCAL CATCH on the southeast coast is sheepshead. Once you see a sheepshead, you will never forget what they look like. This funny little fish has prominent teeth that are reminiscent of those of a sheep. Just picture a fish with dentures! These teeth are the secret to their delicious flavor, because they are vital for crushing the shellfish on which they regularly feast. This diet imparts a particular sweetness to the meat that is almost reminiscent of crab. It's divine. This recipe plays up the beautifully meaty, sweet nature of the fish by slow-cooking it in a very classic mix of butter, lemon, paprika, and parsley. If you can't find sheepshead, look for flounder as a good alternative.

6	(4-OUNCE/115 G) PORTIONS OF SHEEPSHEAD FILLETS
3	TEASPOONS SALT
½	CUP (1 STICK/115 G) BUTTER
2	SHALLOTS, *thinly sliced*
3	CLOVES GARLIC, *thinly sliced*
1½	TABLESPOONS DRY SHERRY
1	LEMON, *½ juiced and ½ sliced into thin rounds*
1	TABLESPOON CHOPPED FRESH PARSLEY
1	TEASPOON PAPRIKA

Preheat the oven to 325°F (169°C).

Season the sheepshead using 2 teaspoons of the salt. Coat a baking dish with 1 tablespoon of the butter. Lay the sheepshead in the baking dish in a single layer.

In a small pot, melt 1 tablespoon of the butter over low heat. Add the shallots and garlic and sauté for 1 minute. Add the remaining butter. When melted, add the sherry, lemon juice, and remaining 1 teaspoon salt. Stir well and pour over the fish. Top the fish with the parsley, paprika, and lemon slices. Bake for 10 to 12 minutes, until cooked through. Serve immediately.

I ENJOY EATING A big bowl of clams for multiple reasons—the most important being you have to use your hands. You simply can't get every little clam, soak up every last drop of broth, unless you use your hands. There are two perfect ways that I have eaten this dish. The first was a cold March day on the beach, accompanied by close friends. Shielding our fire from the wind, the clams were cooked by nestling a pot in hot coals; the Vouvray was used for cooking the clams and drinking. Our hands got messy and we happily ignored the sand that clung to every possible surface. The second was when I cooked this on my home range. I dumped the steamed clams in a very large bowl, toasted up some sourdough bread, and shared it with my best friend. We sat on the floor of my living room, soaking our crusty bread in the fennel-laden broth. Few words were exchanged; there was just focused effort on sussing out every little clam until the bowl was exhausted. No matter where you are cooking, make sure to choose a wine you want to drink with the clams—it's worth it.

Steamed Clams

in Fennel, Lemon, and Cream

SERVES 2 TO 4

2	TABLESPOONS BUTTER
½	FENNEL BULB, *diced small*
3	CLOVES GARLIC, *thinly sliced*
3	POUNDS (1.4 KG) LITTLENECK CLAMS
½	CUP (120 ML) WHITE WINE, *preferably Vouvray!*
½	LEMON, *sliced into thin rounds*
½	CUP (120 ML) HEAVY CREAM
3	TABLESPOONS CHOPPED FRESH CHERVIL
	CRUSTY BREAD

Build a fire and let it burn down to high heat (see Notes).

Put the butter in a Dutch oven or heavy-bottom pot and place directly on the coals. When the butter is melted and bubbling, add the fennel and garlic and cook for 2 to 3 minutes, stirring constantly, until gently caramelized. Add the clams, wine, and lemon slices. Cover and cook until all the clams open, 6 to 8 minutes. Stir in the cream and chervil.

Eat with your hands, some crusty bread, and the rest of your fine wine.

NOTES ON OUTDOOR COOKING
When taking this dish outdoors, make sure to pack a cast-iron Dutch oven, wood for the fire, and three or four towels (for that hot handle!). Plan on eating straight out of the pot, and pack the ingredients already measured out for easy cooking. When cooking over live fire, I find that everything goes a little faster, so keep a little water nearby, in case your liquids are evaporating too quickly.

NOTES ON INDOOR COOKING
If you're staying indoors to cook this dish I still recommend using a Dutch oven. The tight, heavy lid is best for a good seal to keep those clams a-steamin'.

In a Dutch oven or heavy-bottom pot over high heat, add the butter. When the butter is melted and bubbling add the fennel and garlic and cook 2 to 3 minutes, stirring constantly, until gently caramelized. Add the clams, wine, and lemon slices. Cover and cook until all the clams open, 6 to 8 minutes. Stir in the cream and chervil.

Citrus and Herb Roasted Chicken

SERVES 2 TO 4

THE SEASONING FOR THIS CHICKEN is inspired by mojo. Mojo is a sauce that worked its way from the Canary Islands throughout the Caribbean, most famously establishing its identity in Cuban cuisine. The first time I had mojo it was served as a condiment at a small Cuban restaurant in Florida. I took up the charge and doused everything on my plate in it. The waiter thought I had lost my mind. The sauce for this dish is made from the drippings that develop on the bottom of the pan, so make sure you save those juices after roasting. The cook time is shortened by spatchcocking the chicken—removing the backbone—before roasting.

1   (4-POUND/1.8 KG) WHOLE CHICKEN, *backbone removed (see Note)*

1   TABLESPOON OLIVE OIL

4   TEASPOONS SALT

1   TEASPOON FRESHLY GROUND BLACK PEPPER

1   TEASPOON GROUND CORIANDER

1   TEASPOON GROUND CUMIN

1   TEASPOON PAPRIKA

½   TEASPOON CAYENNE POWDER

1   TABLESPOON MINCED FRESH PARSLEY

1   TABLESPOON MINCED FRESH CILANTRO

1   TABLESPOON MINCED FRESH OREGANO

4   CLOVES GARLIC, *smashed*

½   ONION, *cut into wedges*

½   ORANGE, *cut into wedges*

¾   CUP (180 ML) CHICKEN STOCK

Put the chicken in a large bowl and coat it with the oil. In a separate bowl, combine the salt, black pepper, coriander, cumin, paprika, and cayenne.

Season the chicken, back and front, with all of the spice mixture. Sprinkle the parsley, cilantro, and oregano on the chicken. Add the garlic, onion, and orange wedges to the bowl. Cover and place in the refrigerator to marinate for at least 1 hour or up to 8 hours.

Preheat the oven to 375°F (190°C).

In a 12-inch (30.5 cm) cast-iron pan, place the garlic, onion, oranges, and the accumulated juices from the bowl. Pour in the stock. Place the chicken, skin side up, on top of the onion and orange base. Roast for 1 hour, or until the internal temperature reaches 165°F (74°C). Let rest for 10 minutes.

Remove the chicken from the pan and carve into legs, breasts, and wings. Spoon the pan sauce, onion, garlic, and oranges onto a platter. Place the chicken on top and enjoy.

NOTE *Removing the backbone of poultry before cooking is a great way to speed up the cooking process without having to fully butcher your chicken. To spatchcock a chicken, place the whole chicken breast side down on your work surface. If using kitchen shears, start at the base of the spine and cut along the length of the backbone on each side. If using a knife, repeat the same process but begin cutting at the top of the spine and work your way down the backbone. You will be cutting through the rib bones, so it will take some force. Reserve the backbone for stock. Always roast the chicken with the skin exposed to the heat source. In the oven, that would be skin side up, on a grill that would be skin side down, the goal always being crispy, flavorful skin.*

FLORIDA IS FAMOUS FOR its citrus. Every winter, island residents have trees that hang fully weighted with sweet fruit eager to be used. In the kitchen, we are gifted basket after basket of grapefruits and oranges. Dimpled and discolored, the grapefruits are not winning any beauty contests. But cut them open and you are treated to bright pink, tartly sweet flesh that is a joy to keep up with. We run around juicing grapefruits, using them for cocktails, marinades, and of course sweet treats. Inspired by a classic lemon tart, we use island grapefruits, serving each slice alongside local honey and a dollop of chamomile cream.

Grapefruit Tart

with Chamomile Cream and Honey

MAKES
1 (9-INCH/
23 CM) TART;
SERVES 8 TO 10

DOUGH

- ¼ CUP (25 G) SLICED ALMONDS
- 6 TABLESPOONS (45 G) CONFECTIONERS' SUGAR
- 1¼ CUPS (160 G) ALL-PURPOSE FLOUR
- ¼ TEASPOON SALT
- 6 TABLESPOONS (85 G) COLD BUTTER, *diced*
- 2 TABLESPOONS ICE WATER

FILLING

- 3 LARGE EGGS
- 2 EGG YOLKS
- ¾ CUP (150 G) GRANULATED SUGAR
-    ZEST OF 1 GRAPEFRUIT
- 1 CUP (240 ML) GRAPEFRUIT JUICE
- ¼ CUP (60 ML) BUTTERMILK
- 2 TABLESPOONS DRIED CHAMOMILE FLOWERS (see Note)

TO SERVE

- 2½ CUPS CHAMOMILE CREAM (recipe follows)
-    HONEY
-    GRAPEFRUIT SEGMENTS

Preheat the oven to 375°F (190°C).

Make the dough: In a food processor, add the almonds and confectioners' sugar. Pulse until the almonds are finely ground. Add the flour and salt. Pulse to combine. Add the butter and pulse until the butter is well incorporated, about 30 seconds. Add the ice water and pulse until the dough comes together. Transfer the dough to a 9-inch (23 cm) tart pan with a removable bottom. Using floured hands, press the dough into the bottom of the tart pan and up the sides. Use the bottom of a cup measure to smooth and even out the dough. Make sure there are no holes or cracks in the crust. Trim the edges and reserve the scraps. Chill for 30 minutes.

While the dough is chilling, make the filling: In a bowl, combine the whole eggs, egg yolks, granulated sugar, grapefruit zest, grapefruit juice, buttermilk, and chamomile flowers. Whisk to combine. Place in the refrigerator and let steep for 1 hour. Strain through a fine-mesh sieve into a bowl and discard the solids.

Bake the tart shell for 15 minutes, or until light golden brown. Remove from the oven and set aside to cool for 10 minutes. Reduce the oven temperature to 325°F (165°C).

Check the tart shell for any holes or cracks and patch with reserved dough scraps if needed. Place the tart shell on a flat baking sheet and transfer to the oven. Carefully pour in the grapefruit filling and bake until the filling is set, 20 to 25 minutes. Remove from the oven and let cool slightly, about 10 minutes, then place in the refrigerator until cold, about 1 hour.

Serve the tart cold topped with chamomile cream, drizzles of honey, and grapefruit wedges.

Chamomile Cream MAKES 2½ CUPS (600 ML)

- 1½ CUPS (360 ML) HEAVY CREAM
- 5 TABLESPOONS (10 G) DRIED CHAMOMILE FLOWERS (see Note)
- 3 TABLESPOONS CONFECTIONERS' SUGAR

In a small pot, bring the cream to a simmer over medium heat. Remove from the heat and add the chamomile flowers. Steep for 10 minutes. Strain and chill the cream until cold (the cream will not whip if it is not cold). In a bowl, combine the chamomile cream and confectioners' sugar and whip to medium peaks.

NOTE *If you can't find the flowers, you can substitute 2 chamomile teabags to make the tart filling and 5 chamomile teabags to make the chamomile cream. Open the tea bags and empty the contents into the egg mixture or the simmering cream.*

THIS CAKE HAS MAYONNAISE in it. Some of you will read this and think nothing of it. Some of you will read this and think I am crazy. Mayonnaise cakes were born out of the Depression era when ingredients were scarce. In its simplest form, mayonnaise is eggs and oil, which are typical ingredients for ultra-moist cake layers. This particular cake comes by way of an old faded index card from the recipe files of Mary Ferguson. Once a cook in the Greyfield kitchen, Mary is now the managing partner of the inn, and her baking is legendary. This cake is easy to make and rustic in its assembly—essentially a perfect chocolate cake. It is so good that I can't even write this paragraph without craving a slice.

Mary's Double-Chocolate Cake

MAKES 1
(8-INCH/20 CM)
CAKE; SERVES
8 TO 10

- 1½ CUPS (300 G) SUGAR
- 6 TABLESPOONS (30 G) COCOA POWDER (*I use Valrhona*)
- ¾ TEASPOON SALT
- 1 TABLESPOON BAKING SODA
- 1½ CUPS (360 ML) COLD WATER
- 1½ TEASPOONS VANILLA EXTRACT
- 3 CUPS (385 G) ALL-PURPOSE FLOUR
- 1½ CUPS (360 ML) MAYONNAISE, *preferably Duke's*
- 2½ CUPS (600 ML) CHOCOLATE BUTTERCREAM (*recipe follows*)
- 4 CUPS (960 ML) BRANDIED CHERRY WHIPPED CREAM (*recipe follows*)
- DRAINED BRANDIED CHERRIES, *for garnish*

Preheat the oven to 350°F (175°C). Prepare two 8-inch (20 cm) round cake pans by lightly buttering the bottom and sides and lining the bottom with parchment rounds.

In a bowl, mix together the sugar, cocoa powder, salt, and baking soda. Gradually whisk in the water and vanilla. Add the flour and gently stir to combine. Make sure to break up any lumps. Stir in the mayonnaise. Equally divide the batter between the prepared cake pans. Bake for 30 minutes, or until a cake tester inserted in the center comes out clean. Let cool in the pans for 15 minutes. Remove the cakes from the pans and let cool in the refrigerator until ready to assemble.

To assemble the cake, use a serrated knife to trim and level the cake layers. Place one cake layer on a serving platter. Top with the butter-cream, spreading it evenly to the edge of the cake. Add the second cake layer. Top with half of the cherry whipped cream. Refrigerate to set. Remove from the refrigerator 15 minutes before garnishing with whole brandied cherries and serving with the remaining whipped cream on the side. Indulge!

Chocolate Buttercream MAKES 2½ CUPS (600 ML)

- 1⅓ CUPS (165 G) CONFECTIONERS' SUGAR
- 4 OUNCES (115 G) SEMISWEET CHOCOLATE, *melted and cooled to room temperature*
- 1 TEASPOON VANILLA EXTRACT
- 1½ CUPS (3 STICKS/340 G) BUTTER, *softened*

In a bowl, combine the confectioners' sugar, melted chocolate, vanilla, and butter. Whisk for 2 to 3 minutes, until light and airy. Cover and refrigerate until cold but still spreadable, about 5 to 10 minutes.

Brandied Cherry Whipped Cream
MAKES 4 CUPS (960 ML)

- 2 CUPS (480 ML) HEAVY CREAM
- ¼ CUP (30 G) CONFECTIONERS' SUGAR
- 1 CUP (160 G) DRAINED BRANDIED CHERRIES, *chopped*

In a bowl, combine the cream and confectioners' sugar. Whisk to stiff peaks. Fold in the cherries. Use the same day.

HOW TO THROW AN

OYSTER ROAST

BUILD A FIRE

Cook over live fire! Yes, build a fire. How? See page 36. An oyster roast must take place outside. Rain or shine, night or day, mosquitoes or nil. All cooking, eating, and drinking must take place in the great outdoors.

ESSENTIAL EQUIPMENT

- 1 grill loaded with wood or charcoal
- Tongs
- Bucket
- Large table for people to stand around
- 1 towel per person
- 1 oyster knife per person

GOOD OYSTERS

Find the best oysters you can get your hands on. If you live in an oyster-growing region, great. If you live in the Midwest, no problem. Go online and order some. And don't order sparingly; an oyster-loving crowd will plow through your stash. I like to plan on 10 to 15 per person.

THE MORE THE MERRIER

Gather a crowd. Your friends, your neighbors, some people you meet at the grocery store . . . it doesn't matter who it is; part of the fun is the shared table.

GET MESSY

Eat with your hands. Get butter on your fingertips. Dribble oyster juice on your shirt. Do not approach the table like a museum artifact. Don't search out a tiny little fork. Just dig in with your hands . . .

LEARN TO SHUCK

Learn to shuck an oyster. Unsure how? No problem! Roasted oysters are the perfect way to learn to shuck. They are practically open when they come off the grill. If there is a visible opening, use your oyster knife to run along the edge of the shell to open the oyster. If there is no obvious opening, place the tip of your oyster knife into the hinge at the bottom of the shell and gently use leverage to pop the shell open. Need help? Ask the guy at the end of the table that's scarfing down a dozen a minute. You will be a pro in no time.

CUMBERLAND ISLAND OYSTER ROAST

Roasted Oysters, Classic Cocktail Sauce, Sherry Butter SERVES 8

Roasted Oysters

- 1   BUSHEL (100) OYSTERS
- 1½   CUPS (360 ML) CLASSIC COCKTAIL SAUCE (*recipe follows*)
- 1   CUP (240 ML) SHERRY BUTTER (*recipe follows*)
-     SALTINE CRACKERS
-     HOT SAUCE
-     BOWL OF LEMON WEDGES
-     PREPARED HORSERADISH
-     BEER OR CHAMPAGNE OR BOURBON OR WINE OR . . .

Build a fire in a grill and let it burn down to high heat. There should be some flames still flaring up but not an excessive amount. You don't want the oysters to be engulfed by flames.

Throw on enough oysters to cover the area directly over the fire and let them cook for 3 to 4 minutes. The oysters are done when they just start to release some of their liquid and barely start to open. Some will need more time than others, so use the tongs to grab the oysters that are ready. Pile the cooked oysters in the bucket and unload them onto the table. Use the oyster knives to open them, and use the empty bucket for discarded shells.

Eat a gluttonous amount of oysters. Some with cocktail sauce, some dunked in sherry butter, some on a cracker with hot sauce and lemon juice, some with a generous dose of horseradish. Eat them any way you like.

Classic Cocktail Sauce MAKES 1½ CUPS (360 ML)

- 1   CUP (240 ML) KETCHUP
- 6   TABLESPOONS (90 ML) PREPARED HORSERADISH
- 1   TEASPOON WORCESTERSHIRE SAUCE
- ½   TEASPOON TABASCO SAUCE
-    ZEST OF ½ LEMON
- ¼   TEASPOON OLD BAY SEASONING
- 1   TEASPOON MINCED FRESH PARSLEY

In a bowl, combine all of the ingredients and stir to incorporate. Store in the refrigerator for up to 5 days.

Sherry Butter MAKES 1 CUP (240 ML)

- 1   CUP (2 STICKS/225 G) BUTTER
- 4   CLOVES GARLIC, *minced*
- ½   SMALL SHALLOT, *minced*
- 1   TEASPOON SALT
- 2   TABLESPOONS DRY SHERRY
- 1   BAY LEAF

In a small pot, melt 1 tablespoon of the butter over medium-low heat. Add the garlic and shallot. Gently cook for 1 minute, making sure the garlic and shallot do not brown. Add the remaining butter, the salt, sherry, and bay leaf. Heat until the butter is melted and hot. Serve immediately.

SPRING STARTS EARLY IN the coastal South. The mild temperatures and relatively low humidity make for the best days to explore, before the endless summer. The ocean temperatures are cool, and the days are pleasantly warm. There is a need to celebrate the overabundance of vegetables that define this season—we gather around a shared table or pack a picnic to go.

Spring produce is welcomed into the kitchen and requires only minimal preparation to showcase its bright, clean flavors. Crisp lettuces are tossed with sweet local shrimp, peppery radishes are sautéed in butter with tender peas, and spring onions are pleasantly charred over oak and cedar. Herbs and edible flowers dress the plates, taking a cue from the prolific garden. Strawberries come to life while we watch the last of the Florida citrus retreat.

CHAPTER 2

VEGETABLE

SEASON

MARCH—MAY

SALAD OF SPRING HERBS,
FETA, BELDI OLIVES,
CUCUMBER & WALNUTS

ROASTED FENNEL
GRATIN

RICOTTA DUMPLINGS
WITH SWEET PEAS,
BABY CARROTS
& PARMESAN BROTH

STRAWBERRY SEMIFREDDO
AND BENNE SEED
CRUMBLE

SALAD OF SPRING HERBS, FETA, BELDI OLIVES, CUCUMBER, AND WALNUTS

SERVES 4 TO 6

- 2 CUPS (40 G) ARUGULA
- 1 CUP (30 G) MIXED FRESH HERBS: MINT LEAVES, TARRAGON LEAVES, PARSLEY LEAVES, CHERVIL LEAVES
- 2 CUPS (290 G) CUCUMBER *sliced into ¼-inch rounds*
- 1 TABLESPOON CHOPPED FRESH DILL
- ½ TEASPOON MINCED FRESH PARSLEY
- 1 TEASPOON SEA SALT
- 2 TABLESPOONS LEMON JUICE
- 1 CUP (95 G) WALNUTS, *toasted and salted*
- 1 CUP (160 G) BELDI OLIVES
- 6 OUNCES (170 G) FETA CHEESE
- 2 TABLESPOONS OLIVE OIL
- 2 TEASPOONS ZA'ATAR SPICE BLEND
- ½ CUP (120 ML) LEMON HERB VINAIGRETTE *(page 194)*

In a bowl, gently toss together the arugula and herb leaves. Set aside.

In a bowl, combine the cucumber, dill, minced parsley, salt, and lemon juice.

On a platter, in separate piles, place the arugula mixture, the dressed cucumbers, walnuts, olives, and cheese. Drizzle the oil and za'atar over the cheese. Serve with the vinaigrette on the side.

ROASTED FENNEL GRATIN

SERVES 4

- 1 TABLESPOON OLIVE OIL
- 1 LARGE FENNEL BULB, *cut into 8 thin wedges*
- 1 TABLESPOON BUTTER
- 1 TABLESPOON LEMON JUICE
- ¼ CUP (60 ML) CHICKEN STOCK
- PINCH OF SALT
- GRATIN CREAM *(recipe follows)*
- 3 TABLESPOONS HERBED BREADCRUMBS *(page 103)*
- 1 TABLESPOON MINCED FRESH PARSLEY
- 1 TEASPOON ALEPPO CHILE

Preheat the oven to 350°F (175°C).

In a large ovenproof sauté pan or cast-iron pan, heat the oil over medium heat. Add the fennel wedges in a single layer and cook until lightly caramelized, about 3 minutes. Flip the fennel over and cook for another 3 minutes. Add the butter, lemon juice, and stock, bring to a boil, and reduce for 2 minutes. Transfer the pan to the oven and roast until the liquid is evaporated, about 5 minutes. Season the fennel with the salt. Pour the cream over the fennel and top with the breadcrumbs, parsley, and Aleppo chile. Return the pan to the oven and roast for 10 minutes. Serve hot.

Gratin Cream MAKES ¾ CUP (180 ML)

- 1¼ CUPS (300 ML) HEAVY CREAM
- 1 CLOVE GARLIC, *finely minced*
- ¼ TEASPOON SALT
- ¼ TEASPOON FRESHLY GROUND BLACK PEPPER
- ½ CUP (50 G) FINELY GRATED PARMESAN CHEESE

In a small saucepan, bring the cream and garlic to a boil. Reduce the heat to a simmer and cook until slightly reduced, about 5 minutes. Whisk in the salt, pepper, and Parmesan.

RICOTTA DUMPLINGS WITH SWEET PEAS, BABY CARROTS, AND PARMESAN BROTH

SERVES 4 TO 6

- 12 OUNCES (340 G) RICOTTA, WELL DRAINED (see Note)
- ¼ CUP (25 G) FINELY GRATED PARMESAN CHEESE
- SALT
- ¼ TEASPOON FRESHLY GROUND BLACK PEPPER
- 1 LARGE EGG
- ¾ CUP (95 G) ALL-PURPOSE FLOUR, plus ½ cup (65 g) for dusting
- 1 TABLESPOON OLIVE OIL
- 2 CUPS (240 G) BABY CARROTS, sliced into ½-inch (12 mm) rounds
- 2 CUPS (240 ML) PARMESAN BROTH (recipe follows)
- 2 CUPS (290 G) SHELLED SPRING PEAS
- 5 TABLESPOONS (70 G) ROOM TEMPERATURE BUTTER
- 2 TEASPOONS CHOPPED FRESH CHERVIL

In a bowl, combine the ricotta, Parmesan, ½ teaspoon salt, and the pepper. In a separate small bowl, beat the egg, then add it to the ricotta. Sift ¾ cup (95 g) of the flour into the ricotta mixture. Use your hands to knead the flour into the ricotta and the egg, creating a dough. The dough should not be wet and sticky. Add more flour as needed. Be gentle with the dough—too much flour and kneading means dense dumplings. You want them to be airy and light. Gently knead the dough until the flour is fully incorporated into the ricotta and shaped into a log.

Line a baking sheet with a kitchen towel dusted with flour. Place the dough on a floured work surface. Cut the dough in half and gently roll into a rope about ¾ inch (2 cm) in diameter. Cut the rolled dough into ½-inch (12 mm) pieces and lay them on the towel. Refrigerate. Repeat with the remaining dough. Chill for 30 minutes. If you'd like, use a gnocchi paddle to roll each dough round to create ridges. The dumplings can be kept in the refrigerator, until ready to cook, but should be cooked the same day. Fill a pot with salted water and bring to a boil. Reduce the heat to a gentle simmer.

While the water is heating, in a large sauté pan, heat the oil over medium-high heat. Add the carrots and sauté until lightly caramelized, about 4 minutes. Pour in the broth and bring to a simmer. Cook until the carrots are tender and broth has reduced by half, about 5 minutes. Add the peas and cook until tender, about 3 minutes. Remove from heat. Stir in 1 tablespoon butter and add salt, if needed.

While the vegetables are simmering, cook the dumplings: Place half of the dumplings in the simmering water and cook until they begin to rise to the top and are cooked through, about 4 minutes. The cooking time will vary depending on their size. Remove from the pot with a slotted spoon and repeat with remaining dumplings. Toss with the remaining 4 tablespoons butter, the chervil, and salt to taste.

To serve, transfer the dumplings to a large platter and top with the carrots, peas, and broth.

NOTE *The night before you make this, drain the ricotta in a fine-mesh sieve lined with cheesecloth. Weighing down the ricotta by placing a small plate on top will help to remove excess whey. If your ricotta is very wet, it will need more flour and make for denser dumplings.*

Parmesan Broth MAKES 2 CUPS (480 ML)

- 4 CUPS (960 ML) CHICKEN STOCK
- 1 (2-OUNCE/55 G) PIECE PARMESAN CHEESE (including the rind)

In a medium pot, combine the stock and cheese and bring to a boil. Lower the heat to a simmer and reduce by half, about 35 minutes. Strain the broth through a fine-mesh sieve (you should have 2 cups). The broth can be made ahead and stored in the refrigerator for up to 5 days or in the freezer for 1 month.

STRAWBERRY SEMIFREDDO AND BENNE SEED CRUMBLE

SERVES 6

- 2 CUPS (480 ML) HEAVY CREAM
- 6 EGG YOLKS
- ½ CUP (100 G) SUGAR
- ¼ CUP (60 ML) LEMON JUICE
- 1 TEASPOON VANILLA EXTRACT
  PINCH OF SEA SALT
- 1¼ CUPS (300 ML) STRAWBERRY JAM *(recipe follows)*
- ½ CUP (60 G) BENNE SEED CRUMBLE *(recipe follows)*

Whip the cream to stiff peaks and set aside in the refrigerator.

In a medium pot, bring about 1 inch (2.5 cm) of water to a simmer. In a heatproof mixing bowl, whisk together the egg yolks, sugar, lemon juice, vanilla, and salt. Place the bowl over the pot on the stove that has the small amount of simmering water. The water should not touch the bottom of the bowl. Cook, whisking constantly, until the mixture thickens and becomes lighter in color, about 5 minutes. Scrape into an electric mixer bowl. Using a whisk attachment, whip on medium-high speed until cooled to room temperature. Use a spatula and fold in the whipped cream followed by 1 cup (2.5 cm) of the jam.

Pour the mixture into a container and freeze for at least 5 hours before serving.

To serve, scoop semifreddo into bowls and top with a spoonful of the remaining jam and the benne seed crumble.

Strawberry Jam MAKES 1¼ CUPS (300 ML)

- 4 CUPS (575 G) STRAWBERRIES, *hulled and cut in half*
- ¼ CUP (60 ML) DRY RED WINE
- ¼ CUP (50 G) SUGAR

In a medium saucepan, combine all of the ingredients and bring to a simmer over medium-low heat. Cook, stirring often, until thickened and jamlike, about 25 minutes. Transfer to a container and chill before using. The jam can be made ahead and stored in the refrigerator for up to 5 days.

Benne Seed Crumble MAKES 1½ CUPS (185 G)

- ¼ CUP (55 G) COLD BUTTER, *diced small*
- ½ CUP (65 G) ALL-PURPOSE FLOUR
- ¼ CUP (55 G) BROWN SUGAR
- ½ TEASPOON GROUND CINNAMON
- ¼ TEASPOON SALT
- 3 TABLESPOONS BENNE SEED (AN HEIRLOOM VARIETY OF SESAME SEEDS)

Preheat the oven to 325°F (165°C).

In a mixing bowl, combine all of the ingredients. Use your fingertips to mix the butter into the flour until crumbly and the butter is broken into smaller pieces. Spread the crumble on a parchment-lined baking sheet.

Bake, turning the crumble with a spatula a few times, until evenly golden brown, about 15 minutes. Let cool to room temperature. The crumble can be made ahead and stored in an airtight container at room temperature for up to 1 week.

Asparagus and Green Hill Frittata

SERVES 2

I HAVE EGG SUPERPOWERS. I have worked many busy breakfast shifts during my career. Fried, poached, scrambled soft—you name it, I made it. I have always kept a frittata on the menu, having grown to love its ease and simplicity. It is essentially an omelet with one less step—no folding. To this day, frittatas are my favorite way to prepare eggs. To make my frittatas especially decadent, I use Sweet Grass Dairy Green Hill, a double-cream Camembert-style cheese made in Thomasville, Georgia. When I don't have time to think about what's for dinner, I'll whip this up and eat it with a big pile of lettuces.

4   LARGE EGGS

1   TABLESPOON HEAVY CREAM

¾   TEASPOON SALT

¼   TEASPOON FRESHLY GROUND BLACK PEPPER

1   TABLESPOON BUTTER

10   ASPARAGUS SPEARS *(cut in half lengthwise, if thick)*, *woody ends trimmed off*

2   OUNCES (55 G) SWEET GRASS DAIRY GREEN HILL (OR OTHER DOUBLE-CREAM CHEESE), *thinly sliced*

1   TEASPOON MINCED FRESH PARSLEY

Preheat the oven to 375°F (190°C).

In a bowl, whisk together the eggs, cream, ½ teaspoon of the salt, and the pepper. Set aside.

In a medium (8-inch/20 cm) nonstick pan or well-seasoned cast-iron pan, heat the butter over medium heat. Add the asparagus and remaining ¼ teaspoon salt and cook until barely tender, about 2 minutes. Remove the asparagus from the pan. Reduce the heat to medium-low and pour in the egg mixture. Allow the eggs to lightly set before gently moving around with a rubber spatula, being sure to scrape the bottom and sides of the pan. Continue this process until the eggs are fluffy and set but still a little runny on top, about 3 minutes. Remove the pan from the heat and top with the asparagus, cheese slices, and parsley.

Place in the oven. Cook until the eggs are set and the cheese is melted, about 3 minutes.

Slide the frittata out of the pan onto a platter and serve.

Gogo Paloma

SERVES 1

GOGO FERGUSON IS THE BOHEMIAN island queen of Cumberland. She is the great-great-granddaughter of Thomas and Lucy Carnegie. A visit to Cumberland ideally involves a visit to her jewelry shop and, if you're lucky, an invitation over for dinner. She grew up on Cumberland and knows every bend and curve of the island. She is a world traveler, avid bone collector, and treasure hunter. She is a legend. This drink was created for her by the super talented Greyfield beverage director, Christopher Becerra.

2   OUNCES (60 ML) DEL MAGUEY VIDA MEZCAL OR SILVER TEQUILA

2   OUNCES (60 ML) GRAPEFRUIT JUICE

1   OUNCE (30 ML) LIME JUICE

½   OUNCE (15 ML) SIMPLE SYRUP

    ICE CUBES

4   DASHES PEYCHAUD'S BITTERS

4   OUNCES (½ CUP/120 ML) TOPO CHICO OR OTHER SODA WATER

1   GRAPEFRUIT WEDGE

¼   TEASPOON CHILE FLAKES

In a tall glass, stir together the mezcal, grapefruit juice, lime juice, and simple syrup. Add some ice cubes and the bitters and top with the soda water. Gently stir to combine.

Garnish with the grapefruit wedge dipped in the chile flakes.

Springtime Snacks:

Za'atar Whole-Wheat Crackers, Carrot Hummus, Spring Onion Yogurt, and Salted Radish Butter

SERVES 4 TO 6

THE KITCHEN IS MY favorite place to be. At work, at home, it's my comfort zone. A well-worn table is essential to these spaces—the table that everyone sits around, nibbling on snacks, drinking wine, and sharing stories. These snacks are designed with that space in mind. But all of these recipes easily find life in other dishes. The carrot hummus could work with lamb meatballs (page 118), the radish butter could be brushed over a grilled fish (page 275), and the spring onion yogurt would be delectable with poussin (page 122).

Za'atar Whole-Wheat Crackers MAKES 50 (1½-INCH/3.8 CM) SQUARE CRACKERS

1	CUP (125 G) WHOLE-WHEAT FLOUR
1	CUP (125 G) ALL-PURPOSE FLOUR
1½	TEASPOONS KOSHER SALT
1½	TEASPOONS BAKING POWDER
3	TABLESPOONS PLUS 2 TEASPOONS OLIVE OIL
1½	TABLESPOONS ZA'ATAR SPICE BLEND
½	TEASPOON SEA SALT

In a mixing bowl, stir together the whole wheat flour, all-purpose flour, kosher salt, and baking powder. Pour in ½ cup (120 ml) plus 1½ tablespoons water along with the 3 tablespoons oil. Stir together to form a loose dough and turn out onto a work surface. Use your hands to knead the dough for 5 minutes. Wrap the dough in plastic wrap and let rest at room temperature for 1 hour.

Preheat the oven to 425°F (220°C). Line two baking sheets with parchment paper.

Set up a manual or electric pasta roller. Divide the dough into two portions. Lightly roll out the dough with a rolling pin before starting at the widest setting of the pasta roller. Roll out the dough, decreasing in thickness after each pass through the roller, finishing at the number 2 setting (not quite paper thin, but close). Lay the rolled sheet of dough on one of the prepared baking sheets and then repeat for the second dough portion. Divide the 2 teaspoons oil between the two dough sheets and use a pastry brush to cover the surface. Evenly sprinkle the za'atar and sea salt on the dough sheets and use the palms of your hands to press the seasoning into the dough. Cut into 1½-inch (4 cm) squares. (Alternatively, you can bake them in large pieces and break them into smaller pieces after they bake.)

Bake, rotating the pans halfway through, until the crackers are a light golden brown and snap when broken in half, about 6½ minutes. Let cool to room temperature before storing in an airtight container for up to 1 month.

Carrot Hummus MAKES 2½ CUPS (600 ML)

¼	CUP (60 ML) PLUS 6 TABLESPOONS (90 ML) OLIVE OIL
1½	POUNDS (680 G) CARROTS, *thinly sliced*
1	SMALL SHALLOT, *thinly sliced*
2	CLOVES GARLIC, *chopped*
½	RED BELL PEPPER, *chopped*
½	TEASPOON GROUND CORIANDER
½	TEASPOON SMOKED PAPRIKA
½	TEASPOON GROUND CUMIN
¼	TEASPOON CAYENNE POWDER
3	TABLESPOONS TAHINI
1	TEASPOON LEMON JUICE
2	TEASPOONS SALT

In a large sauté pan, heat the ¼ cup (60 ml) oil over medium-low heat. Add the carrots, shallot, garlic, bell pepper, coriander, smoked paprika, cumin, and cayenne. Cook, stirring often, until the carrots are soft and very tender, about 20 minutes. Transfer the mixture to a food processor. Add the tahini, lemon juice, salt, and 2 tablespoons water. Puree while pouring in the remaining 6 tablespoons (90 ml) oil, until smooth. Store in the refrigerator for up to 5 days.

Spring Onion Yogurt MAKES 2½ CUPS (600 ML)

- 1½ TABLESPOONS OLIVE OIL

- 10 SCALLIONS, *thinly sliced* (about 1¼ cups/75 g)

- 3 CLOVES GARLIC, *minced*

- ½ CUP (70 G) SMALL-DICE CUCUMBER

- 1 TABLESPOON CHOPPED FRESH MINT

- 2 TEASPOONS SALT

- ½ TEASPOON GROUND CORIANDER

- ¼ TEASPOON GROUND CUMIN

- 2 CUPS (480 ML) PLAIN GREEK YOGURT

- ½ TEASPOON LIME JUICE

In a small sauté pan, heat the oil over medium-low heat. Add the scallions and garlic and cook gently until soft, about 3 minutes. Remove from the heat and let cool.

In a bowl, mix together the cooked scallion mixture and remaining ingredients. Store in the refrigerator for up to 2 days.

Salted Radish Butter MAKES ABOUT 1 CUP (225 G)

- 4 OUNCES (115 G) TRIMMED RADISHES

- 1 TEASPOON SEA SALT

- 10 TABLESPOONS (140 G) BUTTER, *at room temperature*

- 1 TABLESPOON CHOPPED FRESH TARRAGON

   ZEST OF 1 LEMON

   PINCH OF FRESHLY GROUND BLACK PEPPER

Grate the radishes on the small holes of a box grater and put in a mixing bowl. Mix in the salt and let sit for 30 minutes.

Drain the liquid from the bowl and pat the radishes dry with paper towels. Combine with the remaining ingredients and mix until thoroughly incorporated. Store in the refrigerator for up to 5 days. Serve the butter at room temperature.

A Note on a
GARDEN

Working with a garden is a dream scenario and an incredible challenge for a chef. Due to the isolated nature of Cumberland Island, the only local produce I have easy access to is grown in Greyfield's two-acre garden, just a short walk from the kitchen. As the sole inheritor of the produce grown, it is my job to make sure that we are using every leaf, root, stem, and flower that the garden produces. Produce is harvested daily. Many of the fresh carrots, peppery turnips, and crisp cucumbers are used before they ever see the inside of a refrigerator.

The garden has had a huge impact on my cooking. In my dishes, I learned to pair crops according to the season, seeing that what grows together in the field often works well together on a plate. I learned to deal with abundance and scarcity. There were battles that I won, like managing to work through more than 200 pounds of tomatoes a week for an endless summer. There are battles I lost, like the four rows of basil that grew to 4 feet tall, large-leafed and bitter in the summer heat. I just couldn't get to them fast enough. When the leaves of arugula were riddled with holes from insects in the garden, what did I do? I turned it into salsa verde. When it was time to uproot all of the cabbage for the next round of crops, we made sauer-

kraut. What was going on the plate was predetermined by what was available from the garden.

I grew to love the challenge. Every spring and early summer, I am over-whelmed by the volume of produce yet in August and September, I look long-ingly at the hot, sun-drenched soil in the garden, unable to produce more than a few eggplant and peppers. In early spring, there may be only one or two crops avail-able before the garden bursts to life so I write menus around a few key items like baby lettuces or hakurei turnips. Some-times I have to work against perceptions of seasonality. Seminole pumpkins are ready as early as August, but guests prefer them in the fall. Tomatoes have a second life in early November, but no one seems to appreciate them the same way they were coveted in June.

There is life in vegetables straight out of the soil. Even after just twenty-four hours in a refrigerator, the flavor of a vege-table can change. You have to rely on your instincts to take advantage of produce at its peak. Working with a garden taught me both flexibility and patience, and it is during this process that I have truly learned to be a chef, to create memorable meals from those neat little rows of produce growing steps from my kitchen door.

BAKING A FISH IS EASY. Cooking it at a low temperature in the oven tends to keep the fish moist and flaky, while the seasoned breadcrumbs give it a desired bite. An overabundance of empty pea shells, the remnants of a day of shelling, was the inspiration for this slaw. Grouper is a favored fish along the Atlantic coast, with the season taking hold in April and stretching through the warm spring months.

Slow-Roasted Grouper

with Sugar Snap Pea Slaw

SERVES 4

4	(4-OUNCE/115 G) PORTIONS OF GROUPER FILLET
1½	TEASPOONS SALT
¼	TEASPOON FRESHLY GROUND BLACK PEPPER
1	EGG YOLK
2	TABLESPOONS MELTED BUTTER
½	CUP (40 G) HERBED BREADCRUMBS (recipe follows)
	SUGAR SNAP PEAS SLAW (recipe follows)

Preheat the oven to 325°F (165°C).

Season the grouper with the salt and pepper and place on a parchment-lined baking sheet.

In a small bowl, whisk the egg yolk; while whisking, slowly pour in the butter to emulsify.

Generously brush the top of the grouper with the egg yolk mixture and top each piece with breadcrumbs, lightly pressing them onto the fish. Bake until the fish is cooked through, 12 to 15 minutes. Serve the fish alongside the slaw.

Herbed Breadcrumbs MAKES 1½ CUPS (115 G)

8	SLICES (4 OUNCES/115 G) BAGUETTE OR SOURDOUGH-STYLE BREAD
2	TABLESPOONS OLIVE OIL
	ZEST OF ½ LEMON
1	TEASPOON MINCED FRESH THYME
1	TEASPOON MINCED FRESH PARSLEY
½	TEASPOON ALEPPO CHILE
½	TEASPOON SALT

Preheat the oven to 325°F (165°C).

Cut the bread into small cubes and place on a baking sheet. Bake until the bread is dry and crunchy in the center, 12 to 15 minutes. Let cool to room temperature, then crush into pebble-size pieces using a rolling pin or food processor. Set aside.

In a medium sauté pan, heat the oil over medium-low heat. Add the lemon zest, thyme, parsley, and Aleppo chile. Cook for 30 seconds. Add the breadcrumbs and salt and cook, stirring often, until golden brown, about 4 minutes. Remove from the heat and let cool to room temperature. Store in an airtight container at room temperature for up to 5 days.

Sugar Snap Pea Slaw SERVES 4

3	CUPS (6 OUNCES/170 G) THINLY SLICED SUGAR SNAP PEAS
1	CUP (95 G) THINLY SLICED FENNEL BULB
½	CUP (65 G) THINLY SLICED CARROT
¼	CUP (60 ML) LEMON HERB VINAIGRETTE (page 194)
½	TEASPOON SALT
1	TABLESPOON MINCED FRESH CHERVIL

In a bowl, toss all of the ingredients together. Let macerate for 5 minutes before serving.

The Grand Aioli

SERVES 2

IN THE SOUTH OF FRANCE, the Grand Aioli is a celebration of the growing season, a platter of fresh produce dipped in aioli to be shared. The abundance of produce grown on the southeast coast is worthy of such a celebration. As spring approaches each year, I eagerly await the spicy greens, grassy crisp spears of asparagus, and the sweet, fat little peas that begin to populate the garden. When they arrive in the kitchen, I pile my plate high with as many vegetables as I can find. Spring produce needs little cooking to shine, and this lunch is a way to highlight the versatile southern produce. Cook the veggies you want, leave the others raw, and dip them in a pleasantly spicy aioli. This meal is also perfectly acceptable for dinner.

Calabrian Chile Aioli MAKES 2 CUPS (480 ML)

- 1 CLOVE GARLIC, *minced*
- 8 CALABRIAN CHILES *(packed in oil)*, *seeded*
- 1 LARGE WHOLE EGG
- 1 EGG YOLK
- 1 TEASPOON DIJON MUSTARD
- 1 TEASPOON SALT
- 1 CUP (240 ML) GRAPESEED OIL
- ½ CUP (120 ML) OLIVE OIL
- 1 TABLESPOON CHAMPAGNE VINEGAR
- 2 TABLESPOONS LEMON JUICE

In a food processor, combine the garlic, chiles, whole egg, egg yolk, mustard, and salt. Puree until smooth. With the motor running, slowly drizzle in the oils and process until emulsified. Stir in the vinegar and lemon juice. Store in the refrigerator for up to 3 days.

NOTE *Aioli can also be made by hand—see the method on page 176.*

VEGETABLES AND THOUGHTS ON HOW TO PREPARE THEM

ROASTED ASPARAGUS

Sauté in a pan with a little olive oil and lemon juice until just tender but still crunchy.

ROASTED BEETS

Roast in a preheated oven, covered, with a little water in the bottom of the baking dish until tender. Peel while still warm. See technique on page 118.

MARINATED BABY CARROTS

Sauté in olive oil until lightly caramelized. Let cool and toss with 1 tablespoon Lemon Herb Vinaigrette (page 194).

SWEET ENGLISH PEAS

Blanch in boiling water for about 15 seconds, then transfer to an ice water bath to cool.

ROASTED SPRING ONIONS

Cut bulbs in half and sauté in olive oil until caramelized and tender.

ARUGULA AND NASTURTIUM

Pile generous handfuls of spicy greens and edible flowers raw on a platter.

ON CUMBERLAND ISLAND, THE GARDEN is within eyeshot of my house. I love watching the progression of spring. Slowly baby carrots and D'Avignon radishes start to peek out of the soil. Next, the herb bed flourishes, offering mint, chervil, and dill. Neat little rows of lettuces dense with leaves are a sure sign that spring has arrived. My favorite lettuce, Little Gem, grows in petite clusters that are sweet and crunchy and retain their texture when tossed with marinated shrimp, tart grapefruit, and cucumbers.

Little Gem Lettuces

with Marinated Shrimp, Cucumber, and Grapefruit

SERVES 4

1	BAY LEAF
½	LEMON, *sliced*
1	TABLESPOON PLUS ¼ TEASPOON KOSHER SALT
8	OUNCES (225 G) SHRIMP, *peeled and cleaned*
½	SHALLOT, *minced*
½	CUP (70 G) SMALL-DICE CUCUMBER, *plus* ½ *cucumber, sliced*
2	TEASPOONS CHOPPED FRESH DILL
½	TEASPOON ALEPPO CHILE
1	TABLESPOON GRAPEFRUIT JUICE
2	TABLESPOONS LEMON HERB VINAIGRETTE *(page 194)*
1	HEAD OF LITTLE GEM LETTUCE, *leaves separated and cleaned*
1	GRAPEFRUIT, *segmented*
	PINCH OF SEA SALT

In a medium pot, bring 1 quart (1 L) water, the bay leaf, lemon slices, and 1 tablespoon of the kosher salt to a boil.

Add the shrimp and cook until bright pink and cooked through, about 2 minutes. Drain the shrimp and place in an ice water bath to stop them from cooking further. Drain the shrimp and dice into small, bite-size pieces. Set aside.

In a small bowl, mix together the diced shrimp, the remaining ¼ teaspoon kosher salt, the shallot, diced cucumber, dill, Aleppo chile, grapefruit juice, and vinaigrette. Let marinate 30 minutes before serving.

To serve, spread the lettuce on a serving platter and spoon the shrimp mixture over the leaves, along with the marinade. Top with the sliced cucumber, grapefruit segments, and sea salt.

Grilled Spring Onions

SERVES 4

SPRING ONIONS ARE NOT to be overlooked. Pleasantly mild in comparison to the big white bulbous onions available later in the season, these onions have been harvested early. Gently marinated and thrown on a grill, they are one of my favorite side vegetables.

1	CLOVE GARLIC, *minced*
1	TABLESPOON LIME JUICE
1	TABLESPOON WORCESTERSHIRE SAUCE
1	TEASPOON SMOKED PAPRIKA
1	TEASPOON KOSHER SALT
¼	TEASPOON FRESHLY GROUND BLACK PEPPER
1	TABLESPOON MINCED FRESH PARSLEY
1	TEASPOON MINCED FRESH THYME
¼	CUP (60 ML) OLIVE OIL
1	POUND (455 G) SPRING ONIONS, *cut in half lengthwise, tops trimmed*
½	TEASPOON SEA SALT

In a mixing bowl, whisk together the garlic, lime juice, Worcestershire sauce, smoked paprika, kosher salt, pepper, parsley, thyme, and oil. Add the onions, toss to coat, and let marinate for 1 hour.

Build a fire in a grill and let it burn down to medium heat (see Note).

Remove the onions from the marinade and reserve the excess marinade. Put the onions on the grill grate, cut side down, and cook until nicely charred, about 4 minutes. Flip the onions over and use a brush to baste with the reserved marinade; cook until charred on both sides and tender, 8 to 10 minutes total.

Transfer the onions to a platter, sprinkle with the sea salt, and serve.

NOTE *If you can't cook on a grill, you can use your oven. Preheat the oven to 400°F (205°C). Remove the onions from the marinade and reserve the excess marinade. Heat 1 tablespoon olive oil in a large sauté pan over medium-high heat. Sear the onions, cut side down, until they begin to caramelize, about 4 minutes. Remove the pan from the heat, turn the onions over, and use a brush to baste the onions with the reserved marinade. Transfer the pan to the oven and cook until the onions are tender, about 5 minutes.*

RADISHES GROW INCREDIBLY WELL in the sandy soil of the southeast coast. During spring the garden is overflowing with spicy D'Avignon, bright red Cherry Belle, and snow-white daikon. They tend to be the first crops to signal spring has arrived, and it is my job to use as many as possible. It's a lovely thing to take spicy radishes and sauté them with butter and herbs. Pairing them with sweet peas and delicate flounder make for an easy way to introduce cooked radish into your repertoire.

Pan-Roasted Flounder

with Buttered Radishes and Sweet Peas

SERVES 2

1	CUP (135 G) SHELLED SPRING PEAS
2	(5-OUNCE/140 G) PORTIONS FLOUNDER FILLET
1¾	TEASPOONS SALT
1	TABLESPOON CANOLA OIL
2	TABLESPOONS BUTTER
½	SHALLOT, *minced*
7	RADISHES (ABOUT 4 OUNCES/115 G), *quartered*
2	TABLESPOONS WHITE WINE
1	TEASPOON MINCED FRESH CHERVIL
	DRIZZLE OF CHILE OIL (page 49)

Bring a medium pot of water to a boil.

Add the peas and blanch until bright green and tender, about 20 seconds. Drain and transfer to an ice water bath. Drain and set aside on a towel to dry.

Season the flounder with 1 teaspoon of the salt. In a medium sauté or cast-iron pan, heat the canola oil over medium-high heat. Add the flounder and sear until golden brown, about 3 minutes. Flip the fish over and cook until the fish is cooked through, about 2 minutes. Remove the fish to a plate and cover to keep warm.

While the fish is cooking, heat the butter in a medium sauté pan over medium-high heat. Add the shallot and cook until soft, about 2 minutes. Add the radishes and sauté for 2 minutes. Pour in the wine and reduce for 1 minute. Toss in the blanched peas, the chervil, and the remaining ¾ teaspoon salt. Stir to combine. Remove from the heat.

Divide the buttered peas and radish between two plates, top each plate with flounder and a healthy drizzle of chile oil, and serve.

A Case for
HERBS

Edible flowers and herbs will change the complexity of any dish. Late winter and early spring are the peak growing seasons for an abundant selection of culinary herbs on the southeast coast. When thinking about creating flavor in a dish during spring, my first instinct is to consider herbs. As the growing season wanes in summer and herbs become less prolific, my thought process has to shift to spices (see page 214). I encourage you to experiment in your own cooking. Here is a list of some of my favorites to work with.

HERBS

BASIL—Sweet, peppery anise flavor

BAY LAUREL—Similar to thyme, lightly floral and aromatic

CHERVIL—Mild and delicate, a cross between parsley and tarragon

CHIVES—Grassy with an oniony flavor

CILANTRO—Fragrant and pungent with a complex citrus flavor

DILL—Distinctive strong flavor, slight lemony note

FENNEL FRONDS—Sweet with mild anise flavor

GINGER—Pungent and spicy with a warming effect

LEMON BALM—Delicate herbaceous lemon flavor

LEMONGRASS—A pleasant earthy lemon flavor

LOVAGE—Strong flavor of celery

PEPPERCRESS—Spicy, peppery notes

MINT—Sweet and cooling, slightly spicy

OREGANO—Woodsy and citrusy notes

PARSLEY—Clean fresh grass flavor, easy to use, versatile

PEA SHOOTS—Mild and fresh, sweet lettuce flavor

ROSEMARY—Strong and aromatic with piney notes

TARRAGON—Warming anise flavor

THYME—Versatile and mild, earthy flavor, lots of unique varieties

FLOWERS

BACHELOR BUTTONS—Sweet gentle clove flavor

BASIL FLOWERS—Mild, floral version of basil

CHAMOMILE—Floral, apple-like flavor

CILANTRO BLOSSOMS—Bright and citrusy

NASTURTIUMS—Peppery and mildly spicy

PEA FLOWERS—Fresh, sweet crisp flavor

ROSELLE HIBISCUS—Tart, cranberry, fruit punch flavor

VIOLAS—Gentle, pleasant sweetness

Greens, Eggs, and Country Ham

SERVES 2

WORKING IN A KITCHEN calls for embracing spontaneity. Have an overabundance of herbs? Make green goddess dressing. Need a salad and there is no lettuce in the garden? Use asparagus. Overcook the soft-boiled eggs? Hard-boiled eggs it is! Extra pieces of country ham? Put them in a salad. I have learned to adjust to the moment and enjoy the bevy of ingredients that I have in front of me. This salad is a magic mixing of excess and absence, as so many of the best dishes are. Country ham is a favored ingredient in the South and a tasty addition to any salad. It is made by salting, smoking, and aging ham for anywhere from nine months to two years. It can vary in saltiness, so adjust the seasoning as needed.

KOSHER SALT

1   BUNCH ASPARAGUS, *woody ends trimmed off*

1   CUP (240 ML) BUTTERMILK GREEN GODDESS DRESSING *(recipe follows)*

2   OUNCES (55 G) COUNTRY HAM, *thinly sliced*

4   HARD-BOILED EGGS, *cut into quarters*

PINCH OF SEA SALT

PINCH OF SMOKED PAPRIKA

DILL BLOSSOMS OR CHIVE BLOSSOMS, *if available*

Bring a large pot of salted water to a boil. Cut the asparagus into thirds. Add the asparagus to the boiling water and blanch until bright green and tender, but still crunchy, about 40 seconds. Drain and transfer to an ice water bath to cool. Drain and pat dry.

Spread a healthy amount of the dressing in the bottom of a serving dish. Arrange the asparagus in a pile on top of the dressing, and layer on the ham and eggs. Season the eggs with the sea salt and smoked paprika. Add any herb blossoms you can find and serve immediately.

Buttermilk Green Goddess Dressing
MAKES 1 CUP (240 ML)

½   TIGHTLY PACKED CUP (15 G) FRESH PARSLEY LEAVES

¼   TIGHTLY PACKED CUP (5 G) FRESH MINT LEAVES

2   TABLESPOONS FRESH TARRAGON LEAVES

½   SHALLOT, *sliced*

½   CLOVE GARLIC, *sliced*

1½   TABLESPOONS OLIVE OIL

ZEST OF 1 LEMON

¼   CUP (35 G) CHOPPED CUCUMBER

¼   CUP (60 ML) BUTTERMILK

¼   TEASPOON SALT

6   TABLESPOONS (90 ML) SOUR CREAM

6   TABLESPOONS (90 ML) MAYONNAISE

Bring a small pot of water to a boil.

Blanch the parsley, mint, tarragon, shallot, and garlic in the boiling water for 20 seconds. Drain and transfer to an ice water bath to cool. Drain and squeeze out excess water. Set aside.

In a blender, combine the oil, lemon zest, cucumber, buttermilk, salt, and the blanched herb mixture. Puree until completely smooth. Pour into a mixing bowl and add the sour cream and mayonnaise. Whisk until smooth. Store in the refrigerator for up to 5 days.

HEAT DOMINATES THIS LANDSCAPE. Spring is a short-lived season and should be savored with a little bit of decadence. Polenta is a dish best enjoyed while the nights are still a little cool. Polenta and grits are basically the same thing, but polenta has a finer grind to the corn. I eat a bowl of polenta the way most people eat ice cream, lingering over each spoonful and its buttery and cheesy delights.

Heirloom Corn Polenta

with Braised Mushrooms and Rosemary

SERVES 2 TO 4

- ½ CUP (120 ML) MILK
- 1½ TEASPOONS SALT
- ¼ TEASPOON FRESHLY GROUND BLACK PEPPER
- ¾ CUP (100 G) POLENTA OR COARSE YELLOW CORNMEAL
- ¼ CUP (55 G) BUTTER
- ¼ CUP (25 G) FINELY GRATED PARMESAN CHEESE, *plus more for serving*
- 1½ CUPS (360 ML) BRAISED MUSHROOMS *(recipe follows)*

In a small pot, bring 2½ cups (600 ml) water, the milk, salt, and pepper to a boil. Thoroughly whisk in the polenta and lower the heat to a simmer. Cook, stirring often, until thickened and the polenta is tender, 25 to 30 minutes. Remove from the heat and stir in the butter and cheese. Cover and keep warm until ready to serve.

Spoon the polenta into a serving dish and top with the braised mushrooms. Grate extra cheese over the top, if you like.

Braised Mushrooms MAKES 1½ CUPS (360 ML)

- 2 TABLESPOONS OLIVE OIL
- 1 SHALLOT, *diced small*
- 2 CLOVES GARLIC, *minced*
- 8 OUNCES (225 G) HEN OF THE WOODS (MAITAKE) MUSHROOMS, *broken into small pieces*
- 1 TEASPOON MINCED FRESH THYME
- ½ TEASPOON MINCED FRESH ROSEMARY
- ½ CUP (120 ML) DRY RED WINE
- ½ CUP (120 ML) PUREED CANNED TOMATOES
- ½ CUP (120 ML) CHICKEN STOCK
- 1 TABLESPOON MINCED FRESH PARSLEY
- 1 TABLESPOON BUTTER
- 1¼ TEASPOONS SALT

In a medium sauté pan, heat the oil over medium-high heat. Add the shallot, garlic, and mushrooms. Sauté until the mushrooms start to caramelize, about 5 minutes. Stir in the thyme and rosemary and cook for 1 minute. Pour in the wine and reduce by half, about 3 minutes. Add the tomatoes and stock, bring to a simmer, and reduce by half, about 5 minutes. Stir in the parsley, butter, and salt. The braised mushrooms can be made ahead and stored for up to 5 days in the refrigerator; reheat before serving.

Lamb Meatballs

with Cumin-Roasted Beets and Cilantro Yogurt

SERVES 4

THERE IS A NATURAL rhythm to the seasons, and late spring often makes me crave lamb. The robust flavor of the lamb, imparted by its fat, does not get overwhelmed by aromatic spices. In fact, I reach for just about every spice on my spice shelf when making these meatballs. Virginia is home to Border Spring Farm and shepherd Craig Rogers, who raises, in my opinion, the best lamb in the country.

2	POUNDS (910 G) GROUND LAMB
¼	CUP (55 G) BUTTER, *at room temperature*
1	TABLESPOON SALT
2	TEASPOONS CHOPPED FRESH PARSLEY
2	TEASPOONS ALEPPO CHILE
2	TEASPOONS DRIED OREGANO
1	TEASPOON GROUND CORIANDER
1	TEASPOON SMOKED PAPRIKA
½	TEASPOON SUMAC POWDER
½	TEASPOON GROUND CUMIN
	ZEST OF 2 LEMONS
2	TABLESPOONS OLIVE OIL
2½	CUPS (340 G) CUMIN-ROASTED BEETS *(recipe follows)*
1	CUP (240 ML) CILANTRO YOGURT *(recipe follows)*

Preheat the oven to 350°F (175°C).

In a bowl, combine the lamb, butter, salt, parsley, Aleppo chile, oregano, coriander, smoked paprika, sumac, cumin, and lemon zest. Mix until thoroughly combined. Shape into golf ball–size rounds (you should have about 20 meatballs).

In a large sauté pan or cast-iron pan that can fit all of the meatballs in a single layer, heat the oil over medium-high heat. (If needed, divide the olive oil and meatballs between two pans.) Add the meatballs and sear until browned on the bottom, about 1½ minutes. Roll the meatballs over and sear for another 1½ minutes. When the meatballs are evenly browned, transfer the pan to the oven and roast until cooked through, about 5 minutes. Remove from the oven and serve with the beets and yogurt.

Cumin-Roasted Beets MAKES 2½ CUPS (340 G)

12	TRIMMED BABY BEETS (12 OUNCES/340 G), *scrubbed*
7	SPRIGS OF THYME
1½	CUPS (360 ML) BOILING WATER
1	TABLESPOON OLIVE OIL
¼	TEASPOON GROUND CORIANDER
¼	TEASPOON GROUND CUMIN
¼	TEASPOON SALT
1	TEASPOON MINCED FRESH PARSLEY

Preheat the oven to 375°F (190°C).

Put the beets and thyme in a roasting pan and pour in the boiling water. Cover with aluminum foil and roast for 35 minutes, or until the beets are easily pierced. Remove from the oven (leave the oven on) and set aside until the beets are cool enough to handle, but still hot (this makes peeling them a lot easier). Remove the skin by rubbing the beets with a kitchen towel, one you don't mind getting a little messy.

Cut the beets into bite-size wedges and toss with the oil, coriander, cumin, salt, and parsley. Spread the beets in a single layer on a baking sheet and roast until lightly caramelized, about 7 minutes. Serve hot or at room temperature.

Cilantro Yogurt MAKES 1 CUP
(240 ML)

- 1 TABLESPOON OLIVE OIL
- 1 TIGHTLY PACKED CUP (30 G)
     FRESH CILANTRO LEAVES
- ¼ TIGHTLY PACKED CUP (5 G)
     FRESH PARSLEY LEAVES
- ¾ CUP (180 ML) PLAIN GREEK
     YOGURT
- 1 CLOVE GARLIC
- 1 TABLESPOON LEMON JUICE
- ¾ TEASPOON SALT

In a blender, combine the oil, cilantro, parsley,
half of the yogurt, the garlic, lemon juice,
1 tablespoon water, and the salt. Blend on high
speed until smooth.

   In a small bowl, mix together the cilantro
puree with the remaining yogurt. Store in the
refrigerator for up to 5 days.

Vegetable

PAIRINGS

For me, excitement mounts on the cusp of a newly emerging season. By the end of winter, I can't look at another braising green and long for tender, sweet lettuce. By spring's end, I start avoiding radishes and eagerly eat the first tomatoes. Summer wanes, and I long to build fires to roast sweet potatoes. And the cycle continues.

Each season, natural pairings begin to emerge. Vegetables that grow together make for good bedfellows. Here are a few of my favorite vegetable pairings. Looking for an easy meal? Throw these pairings over a bed of couscous, rice, or pasta, and you have dinner.

SPRING

Peas & Radishes

Fennel & Potatoes

Asparagus & Leeks

Beets & Carrots

FALL

Winter Squash & Kale

Sweet Potatoes & Collard Greens

Spinach & Turnips

Rutabagas & Mustard Greens

SUMMER

Zucchini & Corn

Tomatoes & Cucumbers

Eggplant & Peppers

Okra & Tomatoes

Filet Beans & Summer Squash

WINTER

Cabbage & Turnips

Parsnips & Brussels Sprouts

Cauliflower & Mustard Greens

Broccoli Greens & Carrots

Spring Meat-and-Three:

Roasted Poussin
with Leeks,
Carrots,
and
Asparagus

SERVES 2

A MEAT-AND-THREE is a restaurant that serves classic southern cooking. You pick out your meat and three vegetable sides, have a glass of sweet tea, and top it off with a slice of pie. It can be served cafeteria style or ordered at the counter. The portions are generous, and the intention is good food in a relaxed environment. Roasting a small tender spring chicken and serving it over a bed of lemony asparagus, buttered leeks, and sweet baby carrots is my version of this classic.

2	WHOLE POUSSINS, *about 1 pound (455 g) each*
1	TABLESPOON PLUS ¼ TEASPOON SALT
1	TEASPOON FRESHLY GROUND BLACK PEPPER
1	TABLESPOON CANOLA OIL
1	TABLESPOON BUTTER
1	CLOVE GARLIC, *smashed*
7	SPRIGS OF THYME
2	BABY LEEKS, *sliced (about 1 cup/90 g)*
2	TABLESPOONS WHITE WINE
	FENNEL-ROASTED CARROTS *(recipe follows)*
	LEMONY ASPARAGUS *(recipe follows)*
½	CUP (120 ML) PRESERVED LEMON SALSA VERDE *(recipe follows)*

Preheat the oven to 350°F (175°C).

Split the poussins in half by cutting straight through the breastbone lengthwise. Season with the 1 tablespoon salt and the black pepper.

In a large ovenproof sauté pan or cast-iron pan, heat the oil over medium-high heat. Add the poussins, skin side down, and sear until the skin begins to brown, about 4 minutes. Add the butter, garlic, and thyme and swirl the pan around to distribute evenly. Continue searing the poussins until the skin is golden brown, about 2 minutes. Flip the poussins over and use a spoon to baste some of the hot oil and butter over the skin. Transfer the pan to the oven and roast until the poussins are cooked through, with an internal temperature of 165°F (74°C), about 12 minutes.

Remove the poussins from the pan and set aside in a warm place. Drain all but about 1 tablespoon of the oil and butter from the pan and place the pan back over medium heat on the stovetop. Add the leeks and the remaining ¼ teaspoon salt and cook until the leeks are tender, about 3 minutes. Add the wine to deglaze the pan and stir to combine with the leeks. Remove from the heat.

Plate the poussins on a serving platter along with the leeks, carrots, and asparagus. Spoon some of the salsa verde over the poussins and serve the rest on the side.

Fennel-Roasted Carrots

2	TEASPOONS OLIVE OIL
1	SMALL BUNCH TRIMMED BABY CARROTS (ABOUT 6 OUNCES/170 G)
½	TEASPOON GROUND FENNEL SEEDS
¼	TEASPOON SALT
¼	CUP (60 ML) CHICKEN STOCK

In a medium sauté pan, heat the oil over medium heat. Add the carrots and cook, stirring occasionally, until the carrots are evenly caramelized, about 10 minutes. Stir in the fennel and salt. Pour in the stock and reduce until the liquid is almost evaporated and glazes the carrots. Remove from the heat and keep warm until ready to serve.

Lemony Asparagus

1	TABLESPOON BUTTER
10	ASPARAGUS SPEARS, *woody ends trimmed off, cut into thirds*
¼	TEASPOON SALT
1	TABLESPOON LEMON JUICE
½	TEASPOON CHOPPED FRESH PARSLEY

In a medium sauté pan, heat the butter over medium-high heat. Add the asparagus and salt. Sauté until the asparagus is cooked through but retains a crisp bite, about 2 minutes. Add the lemon juice and parsley. Toss to combine and serve immediately.

Preserved Lemon Salsa Verde MAKES ½ CUP (120 ML)

- ¼ CUP MINCED SCALLIONS

- 1 TABLESPOON MINCED FRESH PARSLEY

- 1 TABLESPOON MINCED FRESH CILANTRO

- 1 CALABRIAN CHILE (PACKED IN OIL), *seeded and minced; or ½ teaspoon chile flakes*

- 1 TABLESPOON PRESERVED LEMON RIND, *minced; or 1 teaspoon grated lemon zest*

- 6 TABLESPOONS (90 ML) OLIVE OIL

- ¼ TEASPOON SALT

- ½ TEASPOON LEMON JUICE

Combine all of the ingredients in a bowl and stir together. The salsa can be made ahead and stored for up to 2 days in the refrigerator. It is best served at room temperature.

KEEPING A COOKIE JAR well stocked in the company of fifty adults is a challenge. At Greyfield, the cookie jar is not just raided by the guests, the intended recipients. It is also easy prey for hungry staff and visiting family and friends. It is the kitchen's job to keep the jar full, and we dream up lots of interesting flavors—like these buttery little cookies perfumed with the last of the island's oranges and ground fennel seeds. They pair especially well with strong espresso and are one of my favorites.

Orange and Fennel Butter Cookies

MAKES
32 COOKIES

- 2 CUPS (256 G) ALL-PURPOSE FLOUR
- 1 TEASPOON BAKING SODA
- 1 TEASPOON CREAM OF TARTAR
- ½ TEASPOON SALT
- 1 CUP (2 STICKS/225 G) BUTTER, *at room temperature*
- ¾ CUP (150 G) SUGAR
- ¼ CUP (60 ML) HONEY
- 1 LARGE EGG
- ZEST OF 2 ORANGES
- 2 TEASPOONS GROUND FENNEL SEEDS
- CONFECTIONERS' SUGAR, *for garnish*

Preheat the oven to 350°F (175°C).

In a small bowl, whisk together the flour, baking soda, cream of tartar, and salt and set aside.

In an electric mixer, use a paddle attachment to beat together the butter, sugar, and honey until light and airy, about 2 minutes. Add the egg, orange zest, and fennel and beat together. Stop the mixer and scrape the bowl with a rubber spatula. On low speed, add the flour mixture and mix until the dough comes together.

Using a ¾-ounce scoop (a heaping tablespoon), portion the dough onto a parchment–lined baking sheet, leaving about 2 inches (5 cm) between the cookies. Bake until the cookies are a light golden brown and crisped on the edges, about 8 minutes. Let cool to room temperature on the pan before serving. Garnish with a dusting of confectioners' sugar. Store in an airtight container at room temperature for up to 5 days.

Buttermilk Tres Leches Cake

with Strawberries in Fennel Sugar

SERVES 12

TRES LECHES CAKE IS NAMED for the "three milks" that are poured over vanilla cake and absorbed. Inspired by the Cuban and Puerto Rican versions I have had in Florida, I use buttermilk, sweetened condensed milk, and coconut milk. Strawberries are a traditional topping and the first berry of spring on the southeast coast, with Florida strawberries available as early as February. Tossing them in fennel sugar gives a hint of anise flavor, without overwhelming the strawberries, adding an herbaceous note to this sweet dessert. I love tres leches so much that I chose it as my wedding cake.

2	CUPS (256 G) ALL-PURPOSE FLOUR
2	TEASPOONS BAKING POWDER
1	TEASPOON GROUND CINNAMON
1	TEASPOON GROUND FENNEL SEEDS
¼	TEASPOON SALT
½	CUP (1 STICK/115 G) BUTTER, *at room temperature, plus extra for the pan*
¼	CUP (60 ML) COCONUT OIL, *at room temperature*
1⅓	CUPS (265 G) SUGAR
4	LARGE EGGS
1	TEASPOON VANILLA EXTRACT
1⅔	CUPS (405 ML) BUTTERMILK
1	(14-OUNCE/420 ML) CAN SWEETENED CONDENSED MILK
1	(13.5-OUNCE/400 ML) CAN COCONUT MILK
1	TABLESPOON DARK RUM
2½	CUPS (600 ML) VANILLA WHIPPED CREAM *(recipe follows)*
2½	CUPS (455 G) FENNEL-SUGARED STRAWBERRIES *(recipe follows)*

Preheat the oven to 350°F (175°C). Butter a 9 by 11-inch (23 by 28 cm) baking dish and line it with parchment paper.

In a bowl, whisk together the flour, baking powder, cinnamon, fennel, and salt. Set aside.

In an electric mixer, use a paddle attachment to beat together the butter, coconut oil, and sugar until light and airy, about 3 minutes. On low speed, beat in the eggs one at a time, stopping to scrape the bottom of the bowl after each addition. Add in the vanilla. With the mixer running on medium-low speed, in three passes, add in the flour mixture and ⅔ cup (165 ml) of the buttermilk, alternating between the two. Mix until incorporated.

Spread the batter in the prepared pan and bake until golden brown and a tester inserted in the center comes out clean, 30 to 35 minutes. Let cool in the pan for 10 minutes.

Combine the remaining 1 cup (240 ml) buttermilk, the sweetened condensed milk, coconut milk, and rum.

Remove the cake from the pan and place it on a cutting board. Use a serrated knife to trim off the edges and the top of the cake to level it. Cut into twelve equal squares and place in a tight-fitting baking dish, leaving just a tiny gap between them. Use a skewer or fork to poke lots of holes in the top of the cake, then pour all of the buttermilk mixture over. Let the cake soak in the refrigerator for at least 4 hours but preferably overnight.

To serve, top each piece of cake with a spoonful of whipped cream and the fennel-sugared strawberries.

Vanilla Whipped Cream MAKES 2½ CUPS (600 ML)

1½	CUPS (360 ML) HEAVY CREAM, *very cold*
2	TABLESPOONS CONFECTIONERS' SUGAR
¼	TEASPOON VANILLA EXTRACT

In a mixing bowl, combine the cream, confectioners' sugar, and vanilla extract. Whisk to stiff peaks. The whipped cream can be stored in the refrigerator for up to 5 days.

Fennel-Sugared Strawberries MAKES 2½ CUPS (455 G)

1	POUND (455 G) STRAWBERRIES, *hulled and cut into quarters*
2	TEASPOONS SUGAR
½	TEASPOON GROUND FENNEL SEEDS

In a bowl, combine all of the ingredients and toss. Let macerate for 30 minutes before serving. Strawberries can be stored in the refrigerator for up to 5 days.

PACK A PICNIC

THE DESTINATION

Choose your own adventure—the *where* is the key to a good picnic. I've thrown store-bought hummus and a turkey sandwich in a backpack and, after a long hike, had the most delectable lunch. It's an earned reward. Throwing a blanket in your back-yard and letting go of the pretense of a dinner table can be equally satisfying. The only rule to a picnic is to eat outside.

THE WEATHER

The spring trifecta: The light gets a little brighter, the days get just a little longer, and the sun gets just a little warmer. Good weather is what lures me outdoors to eat, but a picnic does not have to rely on sun-shine and perfect temperatures. I imagine a foggy, chilly afternoon picnic with a mug of hot soup is just as alluring as finding a shady spot on a hot day.

BASKET

Or backpack, or bag. Choose for comfort and not for looks. If your destination is far away, consider an insulated cooler bag.

THE BLANKET

If you are headed outdoors with a meal in mind, think ahead to where you want to sit. If there is no appointed makeshift table at your destination, bring a blanket, throw, sheet, or towel. A fallen tree or a large boulder is equally suitable.

THE MEAL

At Greyfield, all the lunches are packed as picnics to encourage the guests to get out and explore the island. Packing fifty pic-nics a day has given me insight into what makes a perfectly packable meal. Keep it simple and easy to eat when going on a journey. Anything that you can eat on a cracker is great. Sandwiches are never a bad choice. Plan on eating with your hands, so bring napkins or towels for the cleanup. Pack light in reusable containers. If you're sticking close to home, make a more elaborate meal.

SPRING PICNIC

Roasted Chicken Salad, Spring Vegetables with Buttermilk Green Goddess Dressing, Cumberland Tomme, Nasturtium Lemonade, Za'atar Whole-Wheat Crackers (page 98), Blueberry Galette   SERVES 4

Roasted Chicken Salad MAKES 2 CUPS (420 G)

- 1   POUND (455 G) BONELESS, SKINLESS CHICKEN BREAST
- 2   TABLESPOONS OLIVE OIL
- 1   TEASPOON SALT
- ½   TEASPOON FRESHLY GROUND BLACK PEPPER
- 1   TEASPOON OLD BAY SEASONING
- 7   SPRIGS OF THYME
- 1   CLOVE GARLIC, *minced*
- 1   SHALLOT, *minced*
- ½   CUP (50 G) SMALL-DICE FENNEL
- ½   CUP (50 G) SMALL-DICE CELERY
- ½   CUP (120 ML) MAYONNAISE
- ¼   CUP (60 ML) SOUR CREAM
- 1   TEASPOON MINCED FRESH DILL
- 1   TEASPOON MINCED FRESH PARSLEY
- ½   TEASPOON LEMON JUICE

Preheat the oven to 350°F (175°C).

In a bowl, combine the chicken, 1 tablespoon of the oil, ¾ teaspoon of the salt, the black pepper, and Old Bay. Mix to evenly coat the chicken. Transfer to a baking sheet or dish and top with the thyme sprigs. Roast until the chicken is cooked through, about 18 minutes. Set the chicken aside to cool.

In a small sauté pan, heat the remaining 1 tablespoon oil over medium heat. Add the garlic, shallot, fennel, and celery. Cook gently until soft but not browned, about 4 minutes. Remove from the heat and let cool completely.

Small dice the chicken and transfer to a mixing bowl, along with the fennel mixture. Stir in the mayonnaise, sour cream, dill, parsley, lemon juice, and the remaining ¼ teaspoon salt. Mix to thoroughly combine. Alternatively, mix in an electric mixer with a paddle attachment on medium speed for 1 minute for a lighter texture.

The salad can be made ahead and stored in the refrigerator for up to 5 days.

Spring Vegetables with Buttermilk Green Goddess Dressing SERVES 4

- 10   TO 12 BABY CARROTS, *trimmed and scrubbed*
- 8   TO 10 D'AVIGNON RADISHES, *trimmed and scrubbed*
- ½   CUP (120 ML) BUTTERMILK GREEN GODDESS DRESSING (*page 114*)

Serve the carrots and radishes with the dressing on the side. As easy as that.

Cumberland Tomme
(or the cheese of your choice!)

When packing cheese for a picnic, select a cheese that is semi-soft to hard. A soft triple-cream will not travel as well. Cumberland tomme from Sequatchie Cove Creamery in Tennessee is a semi-firm cheese with a mild and nutty flavor. Count on 1 to 2 ounces (28 to 55 g) per person as a good serving size.

Nasturtium Lemonade MAKES 8 CUPS (2 L)

- ¾   CUP (150 G) SUGAR
- 2   TIGHTLY PACKED CUPS (60 G) NASTURTIUM FLOWERS
- 3   CUPS (720 ML) ICE WATER
- 1   CUP (240 ML) LEMON JUICE

In a medium pot, combine the sugar and 4 cups (960 ml) water and bring to a boil. Remove from the heat and add the nasturtium flowers. Let steep for 10 minutes. Strain through a fine-mesh sieve into a pitcher and mix with the ice water and lemon juice. Chill before serving.

Blueberry Galette MAKES 1
(8-INCH/20 CM) GALETTE;
SERVES 4 TO 6

GALETTE DOUGH

1⅔ CUPS (205 G) ALL-PURPOSE
     FLOUR, *plus extra for
     dusting*

¼   TEASPOON SALT

2   TABLESPOONS GRANULATED
     SUGAR

9   TABLESPOONS (130 G) COLD
     BUTTER, *diced*

1   LARGE EGG

2   TABLESPOONS COLD WATER,
     plus more as needed

FILLING

12 OUNCES (340 G) FRESH
     BLUEBERRIES

2   TEASPOONS LEMON JUICE

1   TABLESPOON CORNSTARCH

¼   TEASPOON GROUND CINNAMON

1   TEASPOON CHOPPED FRESH
     THYME LEAVES

¼   CUP (50 G) GRANULATED
     SUGAR

1   TABLESPOON BUTTER, DICED
     SMALL

1   TEASPOON TURBINADO SUGAR

Preheat the oven to 375°F (190°C).

Make the dough: In a bowl, stir together the flour, salt, and granulated sugar. Add the butter and use your fingers or a pastry cutter to mix it into the flour until it is coarse and pebbly. Separate the egg and set the white aside. In a bowl, beat the egg yolk and cold water together. Add to the flour mixture. Work into a ball, adding a little more water as needed to bring the dough together. Flatten the ball into a disc and wrap and chill in the refrigerator for 30 minutes.

Make the filling: In a bowl, combine the blueberries, lemon juice, cornstarch, cinnamon, thyme, and granulated sugar.

When the dough is ready, dust a large piece of parchment paper with flour. Roll the dough on the parchment into a 12-inch (30.5 cm) round. The dough should be about ¼ inch (6 mm) thick. Be careful not to let any cracks form in the dough. Transfer the parchment with the dough on it to a baking sheet. Place all of the filling in the center of the dough, leaving at least a 1½-inch (4 cm) border. Top the filling with the diced butter. Brush the reserved egg white around the edge of the dough. Fold the edge up and over the fruit, making sure to seal any cracks that may form. Brush the dough with the egg white. Sprinkle the dough with the turbinado sugar.

Bake for 35 minutes. Reduce the oven temperature to 350°F (175°C) and continue to bake until the crust is golden brown and the filling is bubbling, about 10 minutes. Remove from the oven and let set for at least 10 minutes. Serve warm or at room temperature.

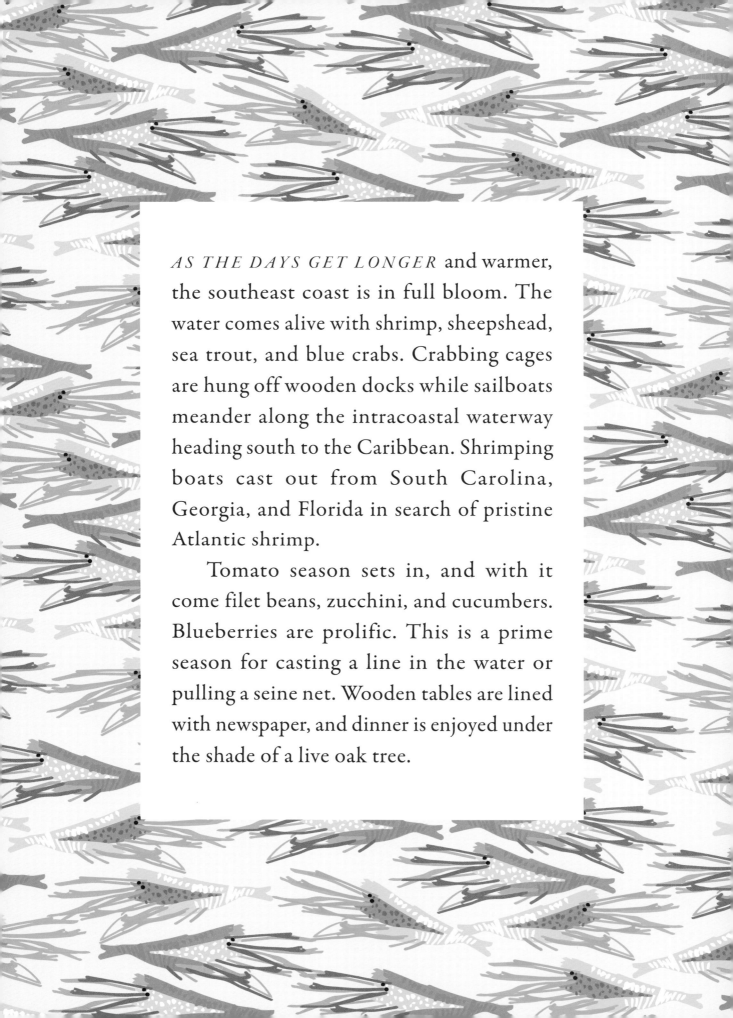

AS THE DAYS GET LONGER and warmer, the southeast coast is in full bloom. The water comes alive with shrimp, sheepshead, sea trout, and blue crabs. Crabbing cages are hung off wooden docks while sailboats meander along the intracoastal waterway heading south to the Caribbean. Shrimping boats cast out from South Carolina, Georgia, and Florida in search of pristine Atlantic shrimp.

Tomato season sets in, and with it come filet beans, zucchini, and cucumbers. Blueberries are prolific. This is a prime season for casting a line in the water or pulling a seine net. Wooden tables are lined with newspaper, and dinner is enjoyed under the shade of a live oak tree.

SHRIMP

SEASON

APRIL–JUNE

Eat more
tropical fruits

Get to know tropical fruits. Mangos, avocados, coconuts, black sapote, papaya, mamey, passion fruit, bananas, and tropical persimmons are just a few of the fruits that grow in Florida. The lush, Caribbean climate of South Florida makes for one of the only tropical growing climates in the United States, setting the region's produce apart.

Here is a guide to eating tropical fruits at their peak. It is important to understand that tropical fruits have very different textures when they are ripe than your average apple or pear. Tropical fruits should be left out at room temperature to ripen. Soft, wrinkled, and muddled brown are often signs of perfect ripeness, not of being spoiled. Throw away any preconceived notions and experiment with something new.

DRAGON FRUIT

RIPE: The outside should be bright pink or red with green artichoke-like scales on the outside. Avoid those with bruises or a sunken-in appearance.

FLAVOR: Crisp in texture, it has a flavor comparable to a kiwi or a mild pear. Very mild and light flavor profile.

TO PREPARE: Trim off the outer stems. Cut in half and scoop out the flesh or cut into half-moons.

MAMEY

RIPE: Brown skin that looks similar to a kiwi. The skin should be slightly wrinkled and soft to the touch. The interior will be a bright, pumpkin-colored orange. The softer, the better.

FLAVOR: Creamy and rich, tastes sweet and complex like a pumpkin pie.

TO PREPARE: Remove the skin. Cube and eat. Makes amazing smoothies.

PAPAYA

RIPE: The fruit will have a slight give when squeezed. The skin will vary from a yellowish green to orange. The flesh color will range from yellow to dark orange, depending on the variety. Florida varieties include Homestead, Betty, and Cariflora.

FLAVOR: Sweet, slightly savory, and lightly acidic.

TO PREPARE: Cut in half and scoop out the seeds; do not eat the skin.

MANGO

RIPE: Vary in color from red to green, orange, yellow, and spotted black depending on the variety. Don't judge the ripeness on the skin color. Feel the mango—the skin should have a slight give when squeezed.

FLAVOR: The fruit will be sweet and juicy, retaining a pleasant firm texture. There are hundreds of varieties, and they each have a distinct flavor. Look for Kent, Glenn, and Haden. If it's grown in South Florida, it's going to taste better. All imported mangos have been dipped in boiling water to kill any fruit flies, impacting the flavor of the fruit. Mango has a high sugar content and high acidity, making it a refreshing treat.

TO PREPARE: Mangos have a flat oval pit that runs along the center. Peel the mango and then cut along the pit from top to bottom. If you hit the pit with your knife, just move over slightly until you can freely slice all the way down.

PASSION FRUIT

RIPE: Sunken in and puckered, they will be purple and yellow in color.

FLAVOR: Sweet and slightly tart, with an incredibly perfumed smell. Think of Hawaiian Punch.

TO PREPARE: Cut in half. The filling is slightly gelatinous with lots of seeds. The seeds are edible. Eat with a spoon right out of the skin.

Tropical Fruit Plate

AN EASY, HEALTHY BREAKFAST option, a plate of tropical fruits is a way to introduce new flavors and taste lots of different varieties. It's fun to compare flavors, mixing and matching familiar items with lesser-known fruits.

SERVES 2

1 BANANA, *sliced into rounds*

1 PASSION FRUIT, *cut in half*

½ ORANGE, *cut into half-moons*

1 HONEY MANGO, *sliced*

½ DRAGON FRUIT, *cut into half-moons*

¼ PAPAYA, *cut into half-moons*

½ SMALL MAMEY, *cut into wedges*

Arrange all of the ingredients on a platter and serve.

A GREAT WAY TO TRY A NEW FRUIT is to pair it with something familiar, like ice cream! Mamey is a fruit native to Cuba and Central America. When ripe it has the texture of roasted sweet potato or pumpkin with notes of vanilla, honey, and chocolate. Fruits like this are so interesting because they do not just hit a sweet note; there is a layer of depth and complexity. It grows in Florida and can be found at grocery stores throughout the state and in specialty stores in Georgia and South Carolina.

1   SMALL MAMEY, *diced*

2   SCOOPS VANILLA ICE
    CREAM

    GROUND CINNAMON

Divide the mamey and ice cream between two small bowls. Dust with cinnamon and serve.

Cinnamon-Dusted Mamey and Vanilla Ice Cream

SERVES 2

IN APRIL AND MAY, with the opening of shrimp season, local shrimping boats are blessed to ensure safe passage and a bountiful catch. These festivals along the southeast coast draw large crowds and rows of white tents slinging every preparation of shrimp imaginable. With these festivals in mind and inspired by the New England lobster roll, I like to make a shrimp salad and pile it high on a soft roll garnished with crisp butterhead lettuce, and eat it along with a handful of crunchy Old Bay potato chips.

Shrimp Roll

with Old Bay Potato Chips

SERVES 6

1	BAY LEAF
½	LEMON, sliced
2	TABLESPOONS PLUS ¼ TEASPOON SALT
1	POUND (455 G) SHRIMP, peeled and cleaned
1	TEASPOON OLIVE OIL
3	TABLESPOONS SMALL-DICE CELERY
2	TABLESPOONS SMALL-DICE FENNEL
1	TABLESPOON SMALL-DICE SHALLOT
½	CUP (120 ML) MAYONNAISE
1	TEASPOON WORCESTERSHIRE SAUCE
¾	TEASPOON TABASCO SAUCE
½	TEASPOON GRATED LEMON ZEST
½	TEASPOON LEMON JUICE
½	TEASPOON CELERY SEED
1	TEASPOON MINCED FRESH CHIVES
1	TEASPOON MINCED FRESH PARSLEY
6	SOFT ROLLS OR HOTDOG BUNS
6	LARGE LETTUCE LEAVES, such as butterhead or Bibb
6	CUPS (170 G) OLD BAY POTATO CHIPS (recipe follows)

In a medium pot, bring 2 quarts (2 L) water, the bay leaf, lemon slices, and 2 tablespoons of the salt to a boil. Add the shrimp and cook until bright pink and cooked through, about 2 minutes. Remove the shrimp and place in an ice water bath to stop them from cooking further. Drain the shrimp and dice into small, bite-size pieces. Set aside.

In a small sauté pan, heat the oil over medium heat. Add the celery, fennel, and shallot and cook until soft, about 2 minutes. Transfer to a bowl and chill until cold.

In a bowl, combine the shrimp, the remaining ¼ teaspoon salt, the chilled celery-fennel mixture, mayonnaise, Worcestershire sauce, Tabasco sauce, lemon zest, lemon juice, celery seed, chives, and parsley. Mix until combined.

Stuff each roll with a leaf of lettuce and ½ cup of the shrimp salad. Serve with a side of Old Bay potato chips.

Old Bay Potato Chips MAKES ABOUT 6 CUPS (170 G)

2	POUNDS (910 G) MEDIUM POTATOES, such as Yukon Gold
½	CUP (120 ML) DISTILLED WHITE VINEGAR
6	CUPS CANOLA OIL
1	TABLESPOON OLD BAY SEASONING
1	TEASPOON SALT

Bring a medium pot of water to a simmer.

Using a mandoline, slice the potatoes into rounds that are ⅛ inch thick and place in a heatproof container. Pour over enough of the simmering water to cover the potatoes and stir in the vinegar. Let the potatoes cool to room temperature. Drain and re-cover with cool water, stirring to release excess starch until the water runs clear, about three passes.

In a medium pot, heat the oil to 325°F (165°C). Combine the Old Bay and salt and set aside. Drain the potato slices and lightly pat them dry with a kitchen towel. Working in batches, add the potatoes to the hot oil. Stir to keep the potatoes from sticking to one another and cook until light golden brown and the bubbles in the oil have subsided. Remove the chips from the oil, transfer to a paper towel–lined baking sheet, and season with some of the Old Bay–salt mixture. Repeat until all the potatoes have been fried.

The chips can be made ahead and stored in an airtight container at room temperature for up to 1 week.

Grilled Coconut Chicken

with Cucumber Jicama Salad and Habanero Coconut Sauce

SERVES 4 TO 6

SPICES HAVE HISTORICAL TIES to Southern cuisine, reflecting the influence of the centuries-old spice trade associated with the British colonies. Country Captain, for example, is a traditional Low County dish with aromatic curry spice and peppers. With growing Caribbean communities, the flavors of the modern South continue to change. This dish is inspired by Jamaican jerk chicken. With the close proximity of the Caribbean, jerk chicken is becoming a staple on menus throughout Florida. The aromatic mixture of allspice, clove, and cinnamon creates a complex marinade infused with the slightest aroma of coconut and wood smoke. I like to pair it with coconut pepper sauce for added spice and a crunchy jicama salad to cool it all down. For an additional image of this dish, see page 30. The coconut pepper sauce is extremely versatile. Try it with roasted cauliflower (page 252), banana leaf–wrapped snapper (page 264), or fried onion petals (page 161).

½ CUP (120 ML) COCONUT OIL

½ CUP (55 G) CHOPPED ONION

3 CLOVES GARLIC, *chopped*

3 HABANERO PEPPERS, *seeded and chopped*

3 TABLESPOONS GROUND ALLSPICE

2 TABLESPOONS FRESHLY GROUND BLACK PEPPER

1 TABLESPOON BROWN SUGAR

1 TEASPOON DRIED OREGANO

1 TEASPOON GROUND CINNAMON

½ TEASPOON GROUND CLOVES

¼ CUP (60 ML) LIME JUICE

¼ CUP (60 ML) COCONUT MILK

2 TABLESPOONS SALT

1 (3½-POUND/1.6 KG) CHICKEN, *cut into legs, thighs, breasts, and wings*

4 CUPS (565 G) CUCUMBER JICAMA SALAD *(recipe follows)*

1 CUP (240 ML) HABANERO COCONUT SAUCE *(recipe follows)*

In a medium sauté pan, heat the coconut oil over medium heat. Add the onion, garlic, and habaneros and cook until lightly caramelized, about 4 minutes. Stir in the allspice, black pepper, brown sugar, oregano, cinnamon, and cloves. Cook, stirring often, until the spices are toasted and fragrant, about 3 minutes. Transfer the mixture to a blender and add the lime juice, coconut milk, and ½ tablespoon of the salt. Blend until smooth. Set aside and let cool to room temperature.

Season the chicken with the remaining 1½ tablespoons salt. Let the chicken rest for 10 minutes to absorb the salt. Transfer chicken to a zip-top bag and add the marinade. Shake the bag to make sure the marinade fully coats the chicken. Squeeze out the excess air. Let marinate in the refrigerator for at least 4 hours or up to 12 hours.

Build a fire in a grill and let it burn down to low heat (see Note).

Remove the chicken from the marinade (the marinade will be solidified because the coconut oil will be cold) and put the chicken on the grill grate, skin side down; cover the grill with the lid. Place the extra marinade in a small pot and warm it on the grill. When the skin is nicely caramelized, flip the chicken over and baste with the reserved marinade. Continue cooking until the chicken is lightly charred and cooked through, with an internal temperature of 165°F (74°C), about 30 minutes (the breasts and wings will probably be done before the legs and thighs).

Serve the chicken on a platter along with the salad and sauce.

NOTE *If you can't cook on a grill, you can use your oven. Preheat the oven to 350°F (175°C). Remove the chicken from the marinade (the marinade will be solidified because the coconut oil will be cold). Set the chicken aside and place excess marinade in a small pot to warm up over low heat. Put 1 tablespoon canola oil in a large cast-iron pan and place over medium heat. When the pan is hot, add the chicken, skin side down, and cook until the skin is nicely caramelized, about 4 minutes. Flip the chicken over and baste with the reserved marinade. Transfer the pan to the oven and cook until the chicken is cooked through, with an internal temperature of 165°F (74°C), 20 to 25 minutes (the breasts and wings will probably be done before the legs and thighs).*

Cucumber Jicama Salad MAKES ABOUT 4 CUPS (565 G)

- 2 CUPS (255 G) PEELED AND DICED JICAMA
- 2 CUPS (290 G) DICED CUCUMBER
- ¼ RED ONION, *thinly sliced*
- 1 TABLESPOON CHOPPED FRESH CILANTRO
- ½ TEASPOON SALT
- 1 TABLESPOON OLIVE OIL
- 2 TABLESPOONS LIME JUICE
- ½ TEASPOON ALEPPO CHILE

In a bowl, mix together the jicama, cucumber, onion, cilantro, and salt. Add the oil, lime juice, and Aleppo chile. Let macerate for 30 minutes before serving.

Habanero Coconut Sauce MAKES 1 CUP (240 ML)

- 2 DRIED GUAJILLO CHILES, *seeded*
- 1 HABANERO PEPPER, *seeded*
- 1 CUP (240 ML) COCONUT MILK
- 2 TEASPOONS LIME JUICE
- ½ TEASPOON SALT

Heat a sauté pan over medium-high heat. Add the dried chiles and toast, moving them around until darkened in color and fragrant, about 1½ minutes. Transfer the dried chiles to a container, cover with hot water, and weigh them down with a plate to keep them submerged. Let soak until soft, about 20 minutes, then drain.

In the same pan over medium-high heat, cook the habanero until soft and blistered in spots, about 3 minutes.

In a blender, combine the soaked chiles, habanero, coconut milk, lime juice, and salt. Puree until smooth. The sauce can be made ahead and stored in the refrigerator for up to 5 days. Serve it at room temperature.

TAKE A ROAD TRIP through Florida and you'll notice roadside signs advertising smoked fish abound. A religion in Florida, fishing has always played an important role in the livelihood of the state's residents, and smoking fish was a way to preserve the day's catch when it didn't sell. Smoked fish dips are my favorite fish camp staple from the region. Mullet is king for Florida fish dips, but this recipe can work with any good-quality smoked fish, from trout to mahi mahi. For more information on how to smoke a fish, check out page 242. Often eaten with saltines, I like to serve mine with hushpuppies.

Smoked Fish Dip

with Hushpuppies

SERVES 4

1   TABLESPOON OLIVE OIL

1   SHALLOT, *finely minced*

1   CLOVE GARLIC, *finely minced*

8   OUNCES (225 G) SMOKED FISH, *skin and bones removed*

2   TABLESPOONS MINCED SCALLION

1   TEASPOON MINCED FRESH DILL

¼   CUP (60 ML) MAYONNAISE

¼   CUP (60 ML) SOUR CREAM

½   TEASPOON FINELY GRATED LEMON ZEST

½   TEASPOON LEMON JUICE

    DASH OF TABASCO SAUCE

    SALT, *if needed*

30   HUSHPUPPIES *(recipe follows)*

Hushpuppies MAKES ABOUT 30

8   CUPS (2 L) CANOLA OIL

1   CUP (120 G) CORNMEAL

½   CUP (65 G) ALL-PURPOSE FLOUR

1   TEASPOON SALT

2   TEASPOONS BAKING POWDER

1   TABLESPOON OLD BAY SEASONING

½   SMALL ONION, *finely diced*

2   TABLESPOONS MINCED FRESH CHIVES

2   TABLESPOON MINCED FRESH PARSLEY

1   LARGE EGG

1½   TABLESPOONS HONEY

¾   CUP (180 ML) BUTTERMILK

In a small sauté pan, heat the oil over medium-low heat. Add the shallot and garlic and cook gently until soft but not browned, about 2 minutes. Remove from the heat and let cool to room temperature.

Tear the smoked fish into smaller pieces and add to an electric mixer bowl, along with the scallion, dill, mayonnaise, sour cream, lemon zest, lemon juice, Tabasco sauce, and the shallot and garlic. Using a paddle attachment, beat at medium speed until fully combined, about 45 seconds. Alternatively, vigorously mix with a spoon for similar results. Taste for seasoning; the saltiness of smoked fish can vary greatly.

Serve with the hushpuppies. Smoked fish dip can be made ahead. Store in the refrigerator for up to 5 days.

In a medium pot, heat the canola oil to 350°F (175°C).

In a medium bowl, mix together the cornmeal, flour, salt, baking powder, and Old Bay. In a separate bowl, combine the onion, chives, parsley, egg, honey, and buttermilk. Stir to thoroughly combine. Pour the wet ingredients into the dry mixture and stir until just combined.

Working in batches, use a ½-ounce scoop or a tablespoon to drop batter into the oil and fry, turning as needed, until deep golden brown all over, 4 to 5 minutes. Transfer the hushpuppies to a paper towel–lined plate. Repeat until all the batter has been fried. Serve immediately, as these are best when still warm.

The Old Man and the Sea

SERVES 1

WITH SMALL PRODUCERS ALONG the southeast coast bringing sugarcane back to the region once known for its production, the South is ready for a rum renaissance. In Charleston, South Carolina, High Wire Distilling Company is producing what it calls Lowcountry Agricole using locally grown, fresh Blue Ribbon Sugar Cane in the style of West Indies *rhum agricole*. Richland Rum, known for its estate grown, single origin production using heirloom Georgia red cane, has two distilleries in Georgia. On Sapelo Island, Georgia, Purple Ribbon Sugar Cane has been revived, being grown for production in cane syrup. Let's hope Sapelo Island Rum is in the future. Inspired by these producers we created a play on the classic Hemingway Daiquiri. The story goes that while living in Cuba, Hemingway frequented El Floridita in Havana, and upon tasting a daiquiri he gave his approval but asked for double the rum and no sugar. Keeping the classic Hemingway in mind, we added a little flaky sea salt and coconut water.

ICE

2   OUNCES (60 ML) WHITE RUM

2   OUNCES (60 ML) GRAPEFRUIT JUICE

2   OUNCES (60 ML) COCONUT WATER

1   OUNCE (30 ML) LIME JUICE

TINY PINCH OF SEA SALT

In a cocktail shaker filled with ice, combine the rum, grapefruit juice, coconut water, and lime juice. Shake well to combine and strain into a rocks glass filled with ice. Sprinkle the salt over the drink.

CUCUMBER SEASON STARTS IN MAY. Pickles, cucumber salads, and roasted cucumbers—I have done it all to keep up with these summer favorites. As the cucumbers grow plentiful in our garden, I am thankful they have a light and crisp flavor that pairs with an endless array of ingredients. Here, olive oil and buttermilk add a pleasant texture and richness, while the Espelette gives it a needed complexity of mild spice and smoke. I like to add small-diced cucumber on top for extra crunch.

Cucumber Buttermilk Soup

SERVES 4

8 CUPS (1.2 KG) SEEDED AND CHOPPED CUCUMBER

1 CLOVE GARLIC, *chopped*

1½ TABLESPOONS SALT

1 CUP (240 ML) BUTTERMILK, *plus extra for garnish*

¼ CUP (60 ML) LEMON JUICE

2 TABLESPOONS CHAMPAGNE VINEGAR

½ CUP (120 ML) OLIVE OIL

ESPELETTE PEPPER

EDIBLE FLOWERS, *for garnish (optional)*

In a bowl, mix together the cucumbers, garlic, and salt and let macerate for 10 minutes.

In a blender, combine the cucumber mixture, buttermilk, lemon juice, vinegar, and oil. Puree until smooth and chill before serving.

Garnish with a drizzle of buttermilk and a pinch of Espelette pepper. Any extra cucumber can be diced small and sprinkled over the top. Edible flowers, such as bachelor buttons, can be used to add a pop of color and flavor.

Welcome to the
LAND OF SHRIMP

"Do you know where I can buy some shrimp?"

Everybody on the southeast coast knows a shrimp guy. There's the guy who sells them out of a cooler, from the side of the road, with a plywood sign spray-painted "Local Shrimp." Every Saturday morning there's the couple at the farmers' market that looks surprised when I ask them to leave the heads on the Mayport shrimp they sell. One time in Thunderbolt, near Savannah, I was directed to a desolate, empty warehouse that housed merely two iced-down coolers full of Georgia whites. On Cumberland, sourcing shrimp is as easy as pulling our boat up next to the local shrimping boat, the *Ashley Michelle*, and loading up a purple mesh bag full of pristine white shrimp.

Supporting local fisherman and buying wild-caught shrimp is a necessity. In the U.S., 80 to 90 percent of all shrimp are imported. Shrimping is a centuries-old industry along the southeast coast that continues to battle against economic hardships and environmental impacts.

Local shrimp are a prized commodity to those that have tasted them. When biting into the sweet, clean white shrimp from the southeast Atlantic coast, you know you are experiencing some of the best shrimp in the world. They spawn and grow in the protective marshes that snake and coil along the intracoastal waterway. The prolific cordgrass helps to define the flavor of the local seafood. A relative of sugarcane, cordgrass imparts a grassy, sweet characteristic to the wild shrimp that this area is famous for.

I've been known to drive more than six hours to pick up a cooler of these shrimp, the flavor is that distinct. Head on, fresh from the salty water, they turn a bright coral pink when cooked and are tasty from head to tail. When buying shrimp, look for wild-caught American shrimp. It pays to ask where your shrimp are coming from. If you need to buy a few pounds while you're on the coast, just ask around; odds are somebody knows a guy around here who can help you out.

Peel-and-Eat
Shrimp

with Smoked
Paprika Butter

SERVES 4

SCATTERED ALONG THE SOUTHERN coast are small towns where shrimp are treated with reverence. Named for the simplistic hands-on approach to eating them, peel-and-eats are a favored preparation from Florida to North Carolina. In my version, the sweet, tender shrimp are complemented by a spice blend of Aleppo, fennel, and coriander and finished with a dunk in the rich and smoky paprika butter. Prepare to get a little messy when eating this iconic dish.

½ ORANGE, *sliced*

7 SPRIGS OF THYME

3 BAY LEAVES

2 TABLESPOONS KOSHER SALT

½ TEASPOON ALEPPO PEPPER FLAKES

½ TEASPOON GROUND CORIANDER

½ TEASPOON GROUND FENNEL SEED

½ TEASPOON SEA SALT

2 POUNDS (910 G) WHOLE HEAD-ON SHRIMP

½ CUP (120 ML) SMOKED PAPRIKA BUTTER (*recipe follows*)

In a large pot, bring 8 cups (2 L) water, the orange slices, thyme, bay leaves, and salt to a boil.

Add the shrimp and cook until the shells are bright pink and the tails have tightly curled, 3 to 4 minutes. Drain the shrimp and transfer to a mixing bowl. Add in the Aleppo pepper flakes, coriander, ground fennel seed, and sea salt and toss to mix. Transfer shrimp to a serving platter and serve immediately with the smoked paprika butter.

Smoked Paprika Butter MAKES ½ CUP (120 ML)

½ CUP (1 STICK/115 G) BUTTER

1 CLOVE GARLIC, *minced*

½ SHALLOT, *minced*

1 TEASPOON SMOKED PAPRIKA

2 TEASPOONS WORCESTERSHIRE SAUCE

¼ TEASPOON SALT

½ TEASPOON ORANGE JUICE

¼ TEASPOON SHERRY VINEGAR

In a small pot, heat half of the butter over medium heat. Add the garlic, shallot, and smoked paprika. Cook gently until soft, about 2 minutes. Add the remaining butter, the Worcestershire sauce, salt, orange juice, and vinegar. Cook until the butter is melted. Serve warm.

A WELL-SEASONED CAST-IRON PAN is essential to any kitchen, which is a lesson I learned cooking in the South. These pans add distinct flavors to the food being cooked in them, and I think they impart a particular texture to vegetables. Filet beans are a variety of green beans that are small and tender. They will pick up just the right amount of char from a cast-iron pan, which imparts a subtle smoky depth and leaves the beans cooked with a retained crunch. This Spanish-inspired *piperade* is a simplified version that I like to keep on hand in the kitchen for everything from topping vegetables to frittatas. A sprinkle of benne seed, an heirloom variety of sesame seed, adds a perfect bit of crunch.

Cast-Iron Filet Beans

Tossed in Piperade and Benne Seed

SERVES 4 TO 6

1   POUND (455 G) FILET BEANS OR GREEN BEANS

1   TABLESPOON CANOLA OIL

1   TEASPOON SALT

1½ CUPS (360 G) PIPERADE (*recipe follows*)

½   CUP (120 ML) CHICKEN STOCK

1   TABLESPOON BUTTER

1   TABLESPOON TOASTED BENNE SEED

1   TEASPOON MINCED FRESH PARSLEY

Piperade MAKES 1½ CUPS (360 G)

3   TABLESPOONS OLIVE OIL

2   RED BELL PEPPERS, *diced small*

½   CUP (65 G) SMALL-DICE ONION

2   CLOVES GARLIC, *minced*

¼   TEASPOON SMOKED PAPRIKA

¼   TEASPOON SWEET PAPRIKA

½   TEASPOON SALT

2   TABLESPOONS CHAMPAGNE VINEGAR

Bring a large pot of water to a boil.

Trim any stems from the filet beans and cut them in half on a bias. Add them to the boiling water and blanch until tender but still crisp, 1 to 2 minutes. Drain and transfer to an ice water bath until cold. Drain and pat dry with a kitchen towel; set aside.

In a large cast-iron pan, heat the oil over high heat. Add the filet beans and shake the pan to evenly distribute them. Let the beans cook until they begin to char, about 1 minute. Shake the pan again and continue to cook until evenly charred, about 3 minutes. Reduce the heat to medium and add the *piperade*, stock, and butter, stirring to combine. Reduce until slightly thickened, about 30 seconds. Remove from the heat. Toss in the benne seeds and parsley and serve.

In a medium sauté pan, heat the oil over low heat. Add the bell peppers and cook gently for 5 minutes, stirring occasionally. Add the onion and garlic and continue to cook for 5 minutes. Stir in the smoked paprika, sweet paprika, salt, and vinegar. Cook for 5 minutes, stirring occasionally. Remove from the heat and set aside until ready to use.

The *piperade* can be made ahead and stored in the refrigerator for up to 5 days.

Zucchini and Crookneck Squash Escabeche

SERVES 4 TO 6

EVERYONE HAS ACCESS TO good zucchini and summer squash, and they are great summertime vegetables that adapt to the flavors they are paired with. I like to toss zucchini in escabeche, an acidic and herbaceous marinade with Latin roots. Charring the zucchini on a grill intensifies and adds depth, making for a flavorful side dish. Easy to make and even easier to serve, this dish is delicious hot, at room temperature, or chilled. I prefer to use baby summer squash when available, as they tend to be a little less watery.

1½ POUNDS (680 G) SQUASH, *preferably baby*

2 TABLESPOONS OLIVE OIL

1½ TEASPOONS SALT

½ CUP (120 ML) ESCABECHE MARINADE *(recipe follows)*

CILANTRO BLOSSOM, *for garnish (optional)*

Build a fire in a grill and let it burn down to medium heat (see Note).

Cut the squash in half lengthwise and toss with the oil and salt. Grill the squash until lightly charred on both sides but still firm in the center, 4 to 5 minutes total. Remove from the grill and let cool to room temperature.

Cut the squash into bite-size pieces (or leave as is if using baby squash) and toss with the marinade. Let marinate for 15 minutes before serving. Garnish with cilantro blossom, if available.

NOTE *If you can't cook on a grill, you can use your stove. Cut the squash in half lengthwise and toss with the oil and salt. Heat a large cast-iron pan over medium-high heat. Add the squash and cook until lightly charred on both sides but still firm in the center, 4 to 5 minutes total. Remove from the pan and let cool to room temperature.*

Escabeche Marinade MAKES 1 CUP (240 ML)

½ CUP (65 G) FINELY DICED RED ONION

1 CLOVE GARLIC, *minced*

½ TEASPOON SALT

¼ TEASPOON FRESHLY GROUND BLACK PEPPER

1 TABLESPOON MINCED FRESH PARSLEY

1 TABLESPOON MINCED FRESH CILANTRO

½ CUP (120 ML) LEMON JUICE

½ CUP (120 ML) OLIVE OIL

In a mixing bowl, stir together the onion, garlic, salt, and pepper. Macerate for 5 minutes. Add the parsley, cilantro, lemon juice, and olive oil and stir to combine.

Escabeche can be made ahead and stored in the refrigerator for up to 5 days.

THIS ONE GOES OUT to all the onion ring lovers out there. These perfectly delicious onion petals manage to retain their crisp bite well after being fried. I like to top them with fried basil and grated Parmesan cheese. A little squeeze of lemon is a pleasant addition. Try serving them with the cilantro yogurt on page 119 or the coconut pepper sauce on page 145.

Crispy Vidalia Onion Petals

with Basil and Parmesan

SERVES 4

4   CUPS (960 ML) CANOLA OIL

1   LARGE VIDALIA ONION, *or other available sweet variety*

1   TABLESPOON PLUS ½ CUP (65 G) ALL-PURPOSE FLOUR

¼   CUP (35 G) CORNMEAL

2   TABLESPOONS CORNSTARCH

¼   TEASPOON BAKING POWDER

1¼   TEASPOONS SALT

½   TEASPOON SMOKED PAPRIKA

½   TEASPOON GARLIC POWDER

¼   TEASPOON FRESHLY GROUND BLACK PEPPER

1   CUP (240 ML) BEER, *lager or ale style*

      SMALL BUNCH OF BABY BASIL

      CHUNK OF PARMESAN CHEESE FOR GRATING

In a medium pot, heat the oil to 350°F (175°C).

Cut the onion in half lengthwise, then cut each half onion into four wedges. Peel off the skin, cut out the root end, and separate into petals. Place in a bowl and toss with 1 tablespoon of the flour. Set aside.

In a mixing bowl, whisk together the remaining ½ cup (65 g) flour, the cornmeal, cornstarch, baking powder, salt, smoked paprika, garlic powder, and pepper. Pour in the beer and mix until just combined.

Working in batches, add the onion petals to the batter and mix to evenly coat them. Using kitchen tweezers or tongs, lift them from the batter and drop them into the hot oil. Cook until golden brown and crispy, about 4 minutes. Transfer to a paper towel–lined baking sheet. When all the onion petals have been fried, add the basil to the oil and fry until crispy, about 15 seconds. Transfer to another paper towel–lined baking sheet.

Place the crispy onions on a serving tray. Use a Microplane to finely grate Parmesan cheese on top and garnish with the crispy basil. Serve immediately.

Blue Crab Ceviche

with Watermelon and Tomatoes

SERVES 4

THE TIDAL CREEKS OF the intracoastal waterway are home to blue crabs, and crabbing is a beloved pastime along the southeast coast. They are easy to spot off the docks and are prized for their sweet and delicate meat. Picking the meat off a blue crab takes time but is worth the work. I like to highlight the sought-after delicate crab meat with buttery, fresh-off-the-vine tomatoes and crisp sweet watermelon. A squeeze of lime and a garnish of fresh cilantro blossoms makes for a bright and complex dish.

16 CHERRY TOMATOES, *cut in half*

2   CUPS (300 G) SMALL-DICE WATERMELON

½   TEASPOON SEA SALT

6   OUNCES (170 G) COOKED BLUE CRABMEAT, *picked over for shells*

½   SERRANO CHILE, *very thinly sliced*

1   CUP (240 ML) WATERMELON MARINADE *(recipe follows)*

1   TEASPOON FRESH CILANTRO BLOSSOMS OR MINCED CILANTRO

2   TABLESPOONS OLIVE OIL

In a small bowl, toss together the tomatoes, watermelon, and salt. Add the crabmeat, chile, and the marinade and fold to combine. Let the mixture marinate in the refrigerator for 1 hour.

Divide the ceviche among four serving bowls and garnish with cilantro blossoms and oil.

Watermelon Marinade MAKES 1 CUP (240 ML)

1   CUP (180 G) CHOPPED TOMATO

1   CUP (150 G) CHOPPED WATERMELON

½   SERRANO CHILE

    JUICE OF 1 LIME (2 TABLESPOONS)

¼   TEASPOON SALT

In a small bowl, combine all the ingredients and let macerate in the refrigerator for 30 minutes.

Transfer to a blender and pulse until almost smooth. Strain the mixture through a fine-mesh sieve into a bowl and discard the solids. Chill before using.

The marinade can be made ahead and stored in the refrigerator for up to 5 days.

THE SIMPLICITY OF COOKING shrimp on the grill never loses its allure. This marinade has a mellow heat that complements the pleasant char from the fire. I like to skewer the shrimp because they are easier to handle once placed on the grill. If you are using wooden skewers, make sure to soak them in water for one hour before using.

1   TABLESPOON COCONUT OIL

2   TEASPOONS MINCED FRESH
     GINGER

1   CLOVE GARLIC, *minced*

6   TABLESPOONS (90 ML)
     SPICY CHILI SAUCE, *such
     as Sriracha*

¾   CUP (180 ML) ORANGE
     JUICE

1   TABLESPOON SUGAR

2   POUNDS (910 G) SHRIMP
     (ABOUT 32), *peeled and
     cleaned*

½   TEASPOON SALT

In a small saucepan, heat the oil over medium heat. Add the ginger and garlic and cook until soft, about 3 minutes. Add the chili sauce, orange juice, and sugar. Stir to combine and bring the mixture to a boil. Reduce the heat to a simmer and cook until slightly reduced and thickened, about 5 minutes. Remove from the heat and let the glaze cool to room temperature before using.

Build a fire in a grill and burn down to medium heat (see Note).

Skewer the shrimp and season with the salt. Place in a dish and toss with the glaze. Grill the shrimp, flipping once, until lightly charred and cooked through, about 5 minutes. Serve immediately.

NOTE *If you can't cook on a grill, you can use your oven. Preheat the oven to 400°F (205°C). Skewer the shrimp and season with the salt. Place in a dish and toss with the glaze. Arrange the shrimp skewers on an aluminum foil–lined sheet pan and place in oven. Cook the shrimp until the tails are tightly curled and the shrimp are cooked through, about 6 to 8 minutes. Serve immediately.*

Ginger and Chile Grilled Shrimp

SERVES 4 TO 6

FISH TALES

Butchering a whole fish can be intimidating. With a little practice, it's a skill anyone can learn. The first time I faced the challenge of butchering a whole fish was early on in my professional career. It was a wild striped bass, about the length of my arm, that weighed between twelve and fourteen pounds. Eager to appear as if I knew what I was doing, I decided to go it alone (note, always ask questions when unsure how to proceed!). My first problem: the scales. The scales were huge. It was me, my knife, and the fish. First, I tried to use the back of my knife. The scales flew everywhere. The table I was working on was small and ill-suited to the size of my fish and the task at hand. I looked around the room frantically. I found a black trash bag and put the fish inside. I used my finger nails to scrape along the trash bag, feeling the scales inside pop off! I must have looked crazy, wildly scraping at this black trash bag for ten minutes, but it worked. I pulled the fish out, and to my satisfaction, most of the scales were gone.

Next the fins, and no kitchen shears at hand! Sweating and doing my best not to cut my fingers off, I was well on my way to ruining this fish. The fins were not going anywhere. I decided to fillet the fish despite the intact fins. Mistake. I knew enough to work along the spine, but my knife kept getting caught on the fins. The meat inside was getting mangled. It took me twenty minutes to work the two fillets free. What was left was a fish carcass with way too much meat intact. The eyewitness to my lack of butchery knowledge was this carcass, and I needed to get rid of him, fast. Fumet! I quickly threw the fish into a stockpot and got a batch of fumet (fish stock) started. I broke down the fillets into four-ounce portions and buried them away until dinner service. Somehow, I managed that entire task with no one checking in on me. Upon the return of the chef I was ruddy-faced and perspiring from embarrassment, but he was none the wiser.

Today I love to butcher fish. I have since learned how to properly break down a fish, without leaving half of the meat attached to the bones. A very sharp knife that is the right size is the most important tool. My favorite knife for everyday use is an eight-inch (20 cm) blade. For butchering fish, I reach for everything from a boning knife to a twelve-inch (30.5 cm) Japanese carbon steel blade. Butchering a flounder is fun; butchering a cobia is a workout. There is always going to be a learning curve, so don't be afraid to mess up. Sometimes, the chef never even notices.

Cumberland Paella

SERVES 6

THE TEMPERATE WATERS DURING this time of year make for a confluence of beautiful seafood. It would be a shame not to bring them all together for at least one dish. Here, sheepshead is matched with the clams and wild shrimp that give the fish its characteristic sweet and flaky meat. Serving the seafood as a paella is a beautiful presentation. I use Carolina Gold rice, but you can opt for a Spanish paella rice; just remember, using different types of rice will change your cooking time. It is important to use your instincts when cooking this dish. The secret to good paella is controlling your heat. You want the liquid to reduce in perfect timing with the rice becoming fully cooked through. Listen to your rice: as the liquid reduces it will lightly sizzle creating the coveted socarrat, which is the crispy, crusty rice at the bottom of the pan that paella fans live for.

12	OUNCES (340 G) SHEEPSHEAD FILLET, *or other mild flaky fish, cut into 6 portions*
18	SHRIMP, *peeled and cleaned, or 12 head-on shrimp, if available*
2½	TEASPOONS SALT
4	TABLESPOONS OLIVE OIL
1	SMALL ONION, *diced small*
1	RED BELL PEPPER, *diced small*
2	SMALL TOMATOES, *diced small*
2	CLOVES GARLIC, *minced*
2	TEASPOONS SMOKED PAPRIKA
1½	CUPS (275 G) CAROLINA GOLD RICE
	PINCH OF SAFFRON
½	CUP (120 ML) WHITE WINE
2½	CUPS (600 ML) CHICKEN STOCK
18	LITTLENECK CLAMS
1	TABLESPOON MINCED FRESH PARSLEY
1	LEMON, *cut into wedges*

Season the sheepshead and shrimp with 1 teaspoon of the salt.

In a large paella pan, heat the oil over medium-high heat. Add the sheepshead and shrimp and sear until light golden brown on both sides, about 3 minutes. Remove the sheepshead and shrimp from the pan and set aside.

To the same pan, over medium-high heat, add the onion, bell pepper, and tomatoes. Sauté, stirring often, until lightly caramelized, about 5 minutes. Stir in the garlic and smoked paprika and cook for 2 minutes. Add the rice along with the remaining 1½ teaspoons salt and the saffron and sauté, while stirring, for 2 minutes. Spread the rice into a flat layer over the entire surface of the pan and add the wine. Cook until the wine is slightly reduced, about 1 minute. Pour in the stock along with 2 cups (480 ml) water. Bring to a simmer and cook for 10 minutes. Do not stir your rice once the liquid has been added.

Add the sheepshead, shrimp, and clams to the pan and lightly press them into the simmering liquid. Continue to cook at a simmer, resisting the urge to stir, until the rice is tender, the liquid has been absorbed and evaporated, and the seafood is cooked through, 12 to 15 minutes (move the pan around on the burner as needed to keep an even simmer). Top with the parsley and serve immediately with the lemon wedges.

I WAS INSPIRED TO START making this dish after traveling and seeing regional versions of rice pudding from France to Cuba. The Southeast is a rice-growing region and this version highlights Carolina Gold rice and the region's strong Caribbean ties. Coconut milk, orange peel, cinnamon, and ginger form the sweet, aromatic base that the rice is cooked in. The whipped cream makes it airy and light. Top with sweet Florida mango and fresh basil.

Carolina Gold Rice Pudding

with Coconut Milk and Mango

SERVES 8 TO 10

1   CUP (185 G) CAROLINA GOLD RICE

3½ CUPS (840 ML) COCONUT MILK

½   TEASPOON GROUND GINGER

½   TEASPOON GROUND CINNAMON

½   TEASPOON VANILLA EXTRACT

    ZEST OF ½ ORANGE

¾   CUP (150 G) SUGAR

2   TABLESPOONS HONEY

¼   TEASPOON SALT

1   EGG YOLK

1   CUP (240 ML) HEAVY CREAM

2   RIPE MANGOS, *peeled and diced*

    SMALL BUNCH OF BABY BASIL

Put the rice in a bowl, cover with cold water, and stir with your hand—the water will turn cloudy from the starch in the rice. Drain the rice in a fine-mesh sieve and return it to the bowl. Repeat this process until the water becomes fairly clear, about five passes. Let the rice drain in the sieve and set aside.

In a small saucepan, bring 1½ cups (360 ml) water to a boil. Stir in the rice and bring back to a boil. Cover, reduce the heat to low, and cook for 15 minutes. Remove from the heat and let stand, covered, for 5 minutes. Remove the lid and fluff the rice with a fork. Set aside.

In a medium saucepan, bring the coconut milk, ginger, cinnamon, vanilla, orange zest, sugar, honey, salt, and 1 cup (240 ml) water to a boil. Stir in the cooked rice and reduce the heat to medium-low. Cook the rice at a gentle simmer, stirring often, until it has absorbed most of the liquid but is still loose, about 15 minutes. Remove from the heat and quickly stir in the egg yolk. Transfer to a wide shallow pan and refrigerate until chilled and set.

Whip the cream to stiff peaks and fold together with the chilled rice pudding. Refrigerate until ready to serve.

Portion the rice pudding into serving bowls and top with the mango and a few leaves of baby basil. Serve cold.

Fresh Blueberries

with Hibiscus and Lime

SERVES 4

THE FIRST TIME I made this recipe was at a dinner party at Canewater Farm, a vegetable farm located in Darien, Georgia. Tamar Adler was writing a story for *Vogue* about Georgia shrimp and had invited me to join her in cooking for a crowd. I made a quick side stop to Harrietts Bluff, a small town with the best organic blueberry farm on the coast. The berries had come into season and I wanted to keep the dessert simple, so I chose to serve them with just a pile of hibiscus cream and lime zest. Sweet blueberries with tart hibiscus is an amazing flavor combination and visually stunning. Never overlook the power of fresh fruit in season as a showstopping course.

2	CUPS (290 G) FRESH BLUEBERRIES
	ZEST OF 2 LIMES *(about 2 teaspoons)*
2	TO 3 TEASPOONS GRANULATED SUGAR
1½	CUPS (360 ML) PLUS 2 TABLESPOONS HEAVY CREAM
7	TABLESPOONS (30 G) DRIED HIBISCUS
¼	CUP (30 G) CONFECTIONERS' SUGAR

Wash the blueberries and remove any stems. Pat the blueberries dry with a towel. Place the blueberries, lime zest, and granulated sugar in a bowl and mix together. (You may need less or more sugar depending on how sweet the berries are naturally.) Refrigerate and let macerate for 1 hour.

Bring 1½ cups (360 ml) of the cream to a simmer and remove from the heat. Stir in the hibiscus and let steep for 10 minutes. Strain the cream through a fine-mesh sieve into a mixing bowl and use the back of a spoon to really press down on the hibiscus to extract all the cream. Refrigerate until cold. Add the remaining 2 tablespoons heavy cream and the confectioners' sugar and whip to stiff peaks.

The hibiscus cream can be made ahead and stored in the refrigerator for up to 5 days.

To serve, divide the cream among four serving bowls and top with the blueberries.

HOW TO COOK A

Low Country Boil

ESSENTIAL INGREDIENTS

A Low Country boil almost always has a dusting of Old Bay, boiled potatoes, sausage, and corn. It may contain one or more types of seafood, but shrimp are the champion of this region. It must have the freshest seafood you can get your hands on—that, my hungry friends, is where the magic lies. On Cumberland, good seafood is always on hand. When shrimp are needed, we can procure sixty to a hundred pounds of head-on Georgia whites, fresh off a shrimping boat.

ESSENTIAL EQUIPMENT

- 1 large stainless-steel pot, preferably one that comes with a perforated basket. The basket makes for easy removal of the ingredients from the cooking water. It's essential for that awe-inspiring moment when you empty the basket of overflowing seafood onto the table.
- For outdoor cooking, a single-burner outdoor stove and a full propane tank
- 1 large spoon with a long handle
- A few kitchen towels
- Lots of newspaper to cover your table

SETTING THE TABLE

Line the table with newspaper. It helps to absorb the excess water that is residual from cooking. It's a tradition and makes for easy cleanup. Remember, no silverware allowed. I love to have warm butter, aioli, and sea salt on hand for eating. A roll of paper towels is a handy addition.

PEELING A HEAD-ON SHRIMP

Pop off the head. Suck the head for the sweet, briny juices. Turn the shrimp on its back and slide your thumb between the legs from head to tail. Peel the outer shell off, letting your thumb be the guide around to the front of the shrimp. Gently squeeze off the tail, because if you pull too quick you will lose the little bit of meat that hides inside.

LOW COUNTRY BOIL

Burnt Lemon Aioli, Cubanelle Pepper Butter

SERVES 8

Low Country Boil

- 4 CUPS (960 ML) TOMATO JUICE
- 4 BAY LEAVES
- 2 LEMONS, *sliced*
- 1 ORANGE, *sliced*
- ¾ CUP (105 G) OLD BAY SEASONING, *plus extra for garnish*
- ¼ CUP (45 G) SALT
- 2 POUNDS (910 G) FINGERLING POTATOES, *cut in half*
- 6 EARS OF CORN, *shucked and cut into 2-inch (5 cm) pieces*
- 1 POUND (455 G) SMOKED SAUSAGE, *such as andouille or kielbasa, sliced about ⅓ inch (8 mm) thick*
- 4 POUNDS (1.8 KG) WHOLE HEAD-ON SHRIMP
- 2 TABLESPOONS MINCED FRESH PARSLEY
- 1¼ CUPS (300 ML) BURNT LEMON AIOLI *(recipe follows)*
- 1½ CUPS (360 ML) CUBANELLE PEPPER BUTTER *(recipe follows)*

In a large pot with a perforated basket, combine 2 gallons (7.6 L) water, the tomato juice, bay leaves, lemons, orange, Old Bay, salt, and potatoes and bring to a boil. Cook until the potatoes are almost tender, about 10 minutes.

Add the corn and sausage and cook until the corn is tender, about 5 minutes. Lower the heat to a simmer and add the shrimp; cook until the shrimp are bright pink and their tails curl up, 3 to 5 minutes. Carefully lift the basket from the pot, being mindful that residual boiling water will drip out. If not using a perforated basket, scoop out the ingredients with a long-handled strainer or drain using a colander.

Transfer the Low Country boil to a newspaper-lined table or large serving platter. Sprinkle with the parsley and additional Old Bay. Serve with the aioli and pepper butter alongside.

Burnt Lemon Aioli MAKES 1¼ CUPS (300 ML)

- 2 LEMONS, *cut in half*
- 2 EGG YOLKS
- 1 TEASPOON DIJON MUSTARD
- 1 CLOVE GARLIC, *finely minced*
- 1 TEASPOON SALT
- ½ CUP (120 ML) GRAPESEED OIL
- ½ CUP (120 ML) OLIVE OIL

Build a fire in a grill and let it burn down to medium heat (see Note). Grill the lemons until lightly charred and caramelized, about 5 minutes. Set aside until cool enough to handle. Zest and juice the lemons into a bowl and set aside. You should have a total of ¼ cup (60 ml) lemon juice.

In a medium bowl, combine the egg yolks, mustard, garlic, and salt. While whisking constantly, slowly drizzle the oils into the egg mixture, starting with just a few drops and gradually increasing to a fine steady stream. Whisk until fully emulsified (if mixture becomes too thick to whisk add in a tablespoon of water to thin out slightly), then add the lemon zest and juice. Store in the refrigerator for up to 3 days.

NOTE *If you can't cook on a grill, you can use your oven. Preheat the broiler on the high setting, place the lemons on a baking sheet, and broil until lightly charred and caramelized, about 5 minutes.*

Cubanelle Pepper Butter MAKES 1½ CUPS (360 ML)

- 1 CUP (2 STICKS/225 G) BUTTER
- 2 CLOVES GARLIC, *minced*
- 1 SHALLOT, *minced*
- 1 CUBANELLE PEPPER, *minced*
- ½ TEASPOON GROUND CORIANDER
- 1 TEASPOON LEMON JUICE
- ¾ TEASPOON SALT

In a medium saucepan, heat half of the butter over medium heat. Add the garlic, shallot, Cubanelle pepper, and coriander. Cook until soft, about 2 minutes. Adjust the heat to low, add the lemon juice and salt, and stir to combine. Melt in the remaining butter and stir to combine. Remove from the heat and keep warm until ready to serve.

THE DAYS ARE LONG, and the nights are warm. These are the hot, humid days of summer, when afternoon thunderstorms abound and loggerhead sea turtles take to the sandy dunes to lay their eggs. Tropical storms are a looming threat along the coastline.

The key to survival in the kitchen is simplicity, eating light. Tomatoes peak in June, but by July the summer heat is so dominant that the only vegetables that thrive are okra, peppers, and eggplant. Peaches come down from Georgia, and mangos head north from South Florida. Honey is harvested from the island bees, fig trees hang heavy with fruit, and chanterelles can be found by heading deep into the maritime forest.

CHAPTER 4

HEAt

SEASON

JUNE—SEPTEMBER

BISCUITS ARE AN ESSENTIAL southern staple, but I can actually say that these biscuits changed my life.

I met Ben working as a line cook in Athens, Georgia. Ben was a pastry chef. It was a relatively small kitchen, so there would be a few days early in the week when it was just the two of us, working and talking. We developed a strong friendship. Every Sunday brunch, Ben was responsible for making buttermilk biscuits. After the biscuits were baked, Ben would offer me one, hot and fresh out of the oven. He would break a biscuit open, and with the flaky layers steaming, he would butter it up and send it my way. As the weeks progressed, Ben started making my biscuits more elaborate. One week it would have melted pimento cheese; the next week was country ham and a fried egg. He would wrap them in foil and pass them across the line to me before service began. Each week it was a new little foil package, thoughtfully assembled. I loved those biscuits. I used to tell him that if he made biscuits for me every day, I might have to marry him. Well, we did get married, and I have since learned to make Ben's biscuit recipe. These biscuits even made it into our wedding vows. Just remember, in the South, mind who you make biscuits for. . . . You may end up marrying them one day.

Ben's Buttermilk Biscuits

MAKES 10 BISCUITS

1   CUP (2 STICKS/225 G) COLD BUTTER, *plus 3 tablespoons melted*

4   CUPS (510 G) ALL-PURPOSE FLOUR, *plus extra for dusting*

2   TABLESPOONS BAKING POWDER

1¼ TABLESPOONS SALT

1¾ CUPS PLUS 2 TABLESPOONS (450 ML) BUTTERMILK

Preheat the oven to 400°F (205°C).

Using the large holes on a box grater, grate the cold butter into a dish and put in the freezer while you gather the rest of the ingredients. You want your butter to be very cold when you mix it with the flour.

In a mixing bowl, sift together the flour and baking powder. Stir in the salt. Add the frozen butter and use your hands to mix the butter into the flour until pebbly in appearance. Pour in the buttermilk and use your hands to form a loose dough.

Lightly dust your work surface with flour. Turn out the biscuit dough and gently work the dough just until it just comes together. Lightly dust a rolling pin with some of the extra flour and begin rolling out the dough until 1 inch (2.5 cm) thick.

Fold the dough into thirds from top to bottom. (Folding the dough will give the biscuits beautiful flaky layers.) Lightly roll out the dough a second time and fold into thirds again, this time from side to side. Roll out the dough to 1 inch (2.5 cm) thick and using a 3-inch (7.5 cm) round cutter, cut out as many

biscuits as you can. Place them on a baking sheet lined with parchment paper. Take the dough scraps, form them back into a ball and roll out to 1 inch (2.5 cm) thick again, and cut out more biscuits.

Brush the melted butter over the tops of the biscuits. Bake the biscuits until they are a beautiful golden brown, 15 to 18 minutes. For my favorite biscuit toppings, turn the page.

NOTE *You can freeze the raw biscuits for another time. Place on a baking sheet and freeze until solid, then package in zip-top bags. You don't need to thaw before cooking; simply place the frozen biscuits on a baking sheet and bake. They will take just a few minutes longer to bake.*

Favorite Ways to Top a Biscuit

THERE IS NO WRONG WAY to top a biscuit. The recipes that follow highlight some of my favorites. Summer fruits, like peaches and figs, grow sweet and ripe in the summer heat and turning them into jam is an easy treat. Slathering a biscuit in honey and butter requires minimal effort. Florida has a reputation for making good honey, with saw palmetto, tupelo, and orange blossom being a few noteworthy varieties.

If you prefer to go with savory options, a fried egg and sharp cheddar is a classic. Ben swears by the combo of grape jelly and breakfast sausage.

Peach and Bay Laurel Jam MAKES 3 CUPS (720 ML)

- 8 LARGE RIPE PEACHES (3½ POUNDS/1.6 KG)
- 1 CUP (200 G) SUGAR
- ¼ CUP (60 ML) SEMISWEET WHITE WINE *(Riesling works great)*
- 2 BAY LEAVES, *fresh or dried*

  PINCH OF SALT

Peel the peaches. Cut in half, remove the pit, and small dice them. In a medium pot, combine the peaches, sugar, wine, bay leaves, and salt. Bring to a gentle simmer and cook, stirring often, until the mixture has become thickened and jam-like, 25 to 30 minutes. Remove from the heat and let cool. The jam can be stored in the refrigerator for up to 1 week.

Fig Jam MAKES 2 CUPS (480 ML)

- 1½ POUNDS (680 G) FRESH FIGS, *stemmed and diced small*
- ¾ CUP (150 G) SUGAR
- 2 TABLESPOONS LEMON JUICE
- 2 OUNCES (55 G) FRESH GINGER, *peeled*

In a medium pot, combine the figs, sugar, and lemon juice. Use a Microplane to grate the ginger into the pot. Bring to a gentle simmer and cook, stirring often, until the liquid has cooked down to a thick jam-like consistency, 40 to 50 minutes. Remove from the heat and let cool. The jam can be stored in the refrigerator for up to 1 week.

Saw Palmetto Honey and Butter ENOUGH FOR 1 BISCUIT

- 1 TABLESPOON BUTTER

  PINCH OF SALT
- 1 TO 2 TABLESPOONS SAW PALMETTO HONEY

Tear a hot biscuit in half. Place the butter and salt in the middle and close. Let the steam of the biscuit melt the butter for 1 minute. Open and spoon the honey over the butter. Eat immediately and repeat.

THERE IS NEVER SUCH a thing as too many tomatoes. They are so versatile. When it's a good tomato year, I am happy to put tomatoes on everything, and an overabundance makes for a great cocktail. The tomato base for this recipe is made with fresh summer ingredients, a spin on a Bloody Mary. But don't stop there. Try using this tomato base with beer or tequila in place of vodka for an easy cocktail.

Heirloom Tomato Bloody Mary

SERVES 6

4   POUNDS (1.8 KG) VERY
     RIPE HEIRLOOM TOMATOES

2   CUCUMBERS (ABOUT
     6 OUNCES/170 G EACH)

4   JALAPEÑOS, *sliced*

1   CLOVE GARLIC, *sliced*

½   CUP (20 G) FRESH
     CILANTRO LEAVES AND
     STEMS

¼   ONION, *sliced*

2   TABLESPOONS
     WORCESTERSHIRE SAUCE

¼   CUP (60 ML) LEMON JUICE

¼   CUP (60 ML) LIME JUICE

1   TEASPOON FRESHLY GROUND
     BLACK PEPPER

1   TABLESPOON KOSHER SALT

     ICE CUBES

6   TO 12 OUNCES (180 TO
     360 ML) VERY COLD
     VODKA, *depending on how
     strong you want your drink*

     SEA SALT *for garnish*

Chop the tomatoes and one of the cucumbers. Combine the tomatoes, chopped cucumber, jalapeños, garlic, cilantro, onion, Worcestershire sauce, lemon juice, lime juice, black pepper, and kosher salt in a bowl. Mix well and let the mixture macerate for 30 minutes.

Working in batches, transfer the tomato mixture to a blender and puree until smooth. Strain through a fine-mesh sieve into a pitcher and set aside; you should have 6 cups (1.4 L) Bloody Mary base. The solids can be kept or discarded (the mixture actually makes for a pretty good salsa).

Fill six 12-ounce (360 ml) glasses with ice cubes. Pour 1 cup (240 ml) of the Bloody Mary base into each glass, followed by your desired amount of vodka (I usually use about 1½ ounces/45 ml vodka in mine). Stir well. Cut the remaining cucumber into 6 spears. Season the cucumber spears with a pinch of sea salt and add a spear to each glass.

The Bloody Mary base can be stored in the refrigerator for up to 5 days or frozen for up to 1 month.

VARIATIONS *Make a Michelada by adding ½ cup (120 ml) Bloody Mary base to an ice-filled glass and top with 1 cup (240 ml) lager-style beer and gently stir them together, or substitute tequila for the vodka for a Bloody Maria.*

Crispy Okra and Tomato Salad

with Feta and Yogurt

SERVES 2 TO 4

EVERYONE NEEDS A PERFECT tomato salad in their arsenal, and this is mine. I started making this at home before it worked its way into the professional kitchen—which is the origin of many of my favorite recipes. The first tomatoes of summer can be eaten without any adornment, so I keep this recipe simple. At the peak of summer, look for bright golden Sungold tomatoes—they are a variety of cherry tomato with a sweet, buttery flavor. The only thing that requires cooking is the okra. The trick is shaving the okra paper thin on a mandoline. Working with a mandoline requires confidence and a sharp blade. Go slow, don't push too hard, and stop when you feel imminent danger. The rewards are worth the risk.

4	CUPS (960 ML) CANOLA OIL
15	MEDIUM OKRA PODS
¾	TEASPOON KOSHER SALT
¼	CUP (60 ML) YOGURT DRESSING (recipe follows)
2	LARGE HEIRLOOM TOMATOES, sliced
12	CHERRY TOMATOES, cut in half (Sungolds! Sungolds! Sungolds!)
1	TEASPOON SEA SALT
2	OUNCES (55 G) FETA CHEESE, crumbled (sheep's milk feta is my favorite)
1	TABLESPOON BENNE SEED, toasted

In a medium pot, heat the oil to 325°F (165°C).

Carefully slice the okra lengthwise, as thin as you can while keeping the pieces intact, using a sharp mandoline.

Add half of the shaved okra to the oil and stir with a slotted spoon to prevent the slices from sticking to one another. Fry until the bubbles have subsided and the white part of the okra has turned golden brown and crispy, about 3 minutes. Scoop out the okra and place on a plate lined with paper towels. Season the okra with half of the kosher salt. Repeat with the remaining okra. Allow okra to cool to room temperature before serving. The okra will stay crispy in an airtight container at room temperature for 2 days.

To assemble the salad, spoon the yogurt dressing along the bottom of a serving plate. Arrange the tomatoes over the yogurt and season with the sea salt. Sprinkle the cheese over the tomatoes. Pile the okra on top and garnish with the benne seed.

Yogurt Dressing

MAKES ½ CUP (120 ML)

½	CUP (120 ML) PLAIN YOGURT
	PINCH OF SALT
½	TEASPOON GROUND CORIANDER
½	TEASPOON GROUND CUMIN
½	TEASPOON PAPRIKA
2	TEASPOON LEMON JUICE

In a bowl, whisk together all the ingredients. The dressing can be stored in the refrigerator for up to 5 days.

EGGPLANTS STAND UP TO the heat of summer. After I recover from the sheer joy of tomatoes being back in season, my focus shifts to eggplants. As a chef I challenge myself to stay within the confines of the season, and eggplant has proven to be an inspiration year after year. Smoked, it takes on a rich and luscious texture; roasted in olive oil and sea salt, it caramelizes and intensifies; whipped with tart lemon and creamy yogurt, it becomes silky smooth. This little handheld tart marries the flavors of luscious eggplant, meaty oil-cured Beldi olives, and sweet peppers.

Savory Summer Tarts

of Eggplant, Peppers, and Olives

MAKES 8 SMALL TARTS

¼ CUP (60 ML) OLIVE OIL, *plus 1 tablespoon*

2 EGGPLANTS (ABOUT 1½ POUNDS/680 G), *peeled and diced small*

1 CLOVE GARLIC, *minced*

2½ TEASPOONS SALT

2 CUPS (290 G) SMALL-DICE RED BELL PEPPERS

½ CUP (65 G) SMALL-DICE ONION

¼ TEASPOON ALEPPO CHILE

¼ TEASPOON SHERRY VINEGAR

8 (5-INCH/12 CM) ROUNDS OF SAVORY PIE DOUGH (*recipe follows*), *chilled*

¼ CUP (40 G) PITTED AND CHOPPED BELDI OLIVES

¼ CUP (25 G) FINELY GRATED PARMESAN CHEESE

2 TABLESPOONS CHOPPED FRESH PARSLEY

1 EGG

Preheat the oven to 350°F (175°C).

In a large sauté pan, heat ¼ cup (60 ml) of the oil over medium heat. Add the eggplant, garlic, and 2 teaspoons of the salt. Cook, stirring often, until the eggplant breaks down and caramelizes, about 25 minutes. Use a spoon to lightly mash to a smooth consistency. Remove the eggplant mixture from the pan and set aside.

In a medium sauté pan over medium heat, heat 1 tablespoon of the oil. Add the bell peppers and onion and cook for 2 to 3 minutes, stirring occasionally. Add the remaining ½ teaspoon salt and the Aleppo chile and cook for 2 minutes. Add the vinegar and stir. Remove from the heat and let cool. Set aside for assembly.

On a lightly floured work surface, lay the dough rounds flat and equally distribute the eggplant mixture among the rounds, placing the filling in the center and leaving at least a 1-inch (2.5 cm) border. Equally distribute the pepper mixture among the rounds, placing it on top of the eggplant. Top the eggplant with the olives, cheese, and parsley.

Whisk the egg with 1 tablespoon water to make an egg wash. Spread a small amount of the egg wash along the edge of each pie round and fold the edge up and over the filling, making sure to seal any cracks that may form.

Transfer the pies to a parchment-lined baking sheet and brush with the remaining egg wash. Bake for 22 to 25 minutes, or until the crust is a deep golden brown.

Savory Pie Dough MAKES 8 (5-INCH/12 CM) ROUNDS

2 CUPS (255 G) ALL-PURPOSE FLOUR, *plus extra for dusting*

2 TEASPOONS SALT

1 TEASPOON GROUND CUMIN

1½ TEASPOONS CRUSHED DRIED OREGANO

¾ CUP (1½ STICKS/170 G) COLD BUTTER, *diced small*

6 TABLESPOONS (90 ML) COLD WATER

In a bowl, mix the flour, salt, cumin, and oregano. Mix in the butter using your fingertips or a pastry cutter until coarse and pebbly. Add the water and gently knead the dough together. Add more water as needed to bring the dough together. Shape into a ball and wrap in plastic wrap, flatten into a disc, and refrigerate for 30 minutes.

Lightly dust your work surface with flour and roll out the dough to about ⅛ inch (3 mm) thick. Use the top of a blender or something similar as a guide to cut the dough into 5-inch (12 cm) rounds. Lay the rounds on a baking sheet lined with parchment paper and refrigerate until ready to use. As you fill them, they will return to room temperature, which will make folding the sides easier.

Beach Snacks:

Shrimp
Escabeche
with Sungold
Tomatoes,
Shishito Peppers
with Lime
and Sea Salt,
Coconut
Cashews,
Mango with
Cilantro and
Chile

SERVES 4

THERE IS A SLIGHTLY SWEET COMMONALITY that these menu items share, with the hope that just a little residual saltwater will still be lingering on your lips as you eat. When packing for a meal at the beach, keep it simple. I like to bring a sizable blanket for the feast, food stored in easily resealable jars or tiffin boxes, napkins, and plenty of water. Finger foods are ideal, as there will be less cleanup when you get home. The memory should be the adventure of a shared meal by the ocean, not the fuss of preparation.

Shrimp Escabeche with Sungold Tomatoes

½   LEMON, *sliced*

2   BAY LEAVES

     SMALL HANDFUL OF FRESH THYME

2   TABLESPOONS KOSHER SALT

1½   POUNDS (680 G) SHRIMP, *peeled and deveined*

16   SUNGOLD TOMATOES, *or other cherry tomato variety, cut in halves*

     PINCH OF SEA SALT

1   CUP (240 ML) ESCABECHE MARINADE *(page 158)*

     BABY BASIL

In a large pot, bring 8 cups (2 L) water, the lemon, bay leaves, thyme, and kosher salt to a boil over high heat. Add the shrimp and cook until bright pink and the tails have curled, about 2 minutes. Drain the shrimp and shock them in ice water to cool. Remove the shrimp from the water and toss together with the tomatoes, sea salt, and marinade. Refrigerate until ready to serve. Top with basil.

Shishito Peppers with Lime and Sea Salt

1   TABLESPOON OLIVE OIL

1   POUND (455 G) SHISHITO PEPPERS

1   TABLESPOON LIME JUICE

1½   TEASPOONS SEA SALT

In a large sauté pan, heat the oil over high heat. Add the peppers and sauté until blistered in spots, about 3 minutes. Transfer to a mixing bowl and toss together with the lime juice and salt. Serve warm or at room temperature.

Coconut Cashews

1   TABLESPOON COCONUT OIL

1   TABLESPOON HONEY

6   TABLESPOONS (30 G) SWEETENED COCONUT FLAKES

8   OUNCES (225 G) WHOLE UNSALTED CASHEWS, *toasted*

¾   TEASPOON SALT

Preheat the oven to 325°F (165°C).

In a large sauté pan, heat the coconut oil and honey over medium heat. Add the coconut flakes, cashews, and salt. Mix well. Turn out onto a parchment-lined baking sheet. Bake until the coconut flakes are toasted and an even golden brown, about 8 minutes. Let cool to room temperature before serving. The cashews can be made ahead and stored in an airtight container at room temperature for up to 1 week.

Mango with Cilantro and Chile

- 2 RIPE MANGOS, PEELED AND DICED
- 2 TABLESPOONS CHOPPED FRESH CILANTRO
- 2 TABLESPOONS LIME JUICE
- 2 TABLESPOONS PICKLED RED ONION *(page 277)*
- 1 TEASPOON ALEPPO CHILE

In a mixing bowl, toss together the mango, cilantro, and lime juice. Transfer to a serving dish, top with the pickled onion and Aleppo chile, and serve.

Summary Salad

of
Pole Beans,
Potatoes,
and Pickled Red
Onion

SERVES 2 TO 4

POLE BEANS GET THEIR NAME from the way they grow, requiring a trellis or a pole to climb. Two of my favorite varieties are romano and rattlesnake, which do well in the sandy soil of the coast. When lettuces are limited, using alternative vegetables like pole beans are a great way to build a salad. This dish can be served cold or at room temperature. During the summer, the garden is still producing a variety of micro-greens, including arugula, basil, and mustard. A small handful can pack a pleasant punch. Look for petite greens available from local farmers or at the grocery store to garnish your salad.

3	TABLESPOONS SALT
8	OUNCES (225 G) FINGERLING POTATOES, *sliced ¼ inch (6 mm) thick*
8	OUNCES (225 G) POLE BEANS, *trimmed and cut into bite-size pieces*
½	SERRANO CHILE, *thinly sliced*
¼	CUP (30 G) PICKLED RED ONION *(page 277)*
6	TABLESPOONS (90 ML) LEMON HERB VINAIGRETTE *(recipe follows)*
¼	CUP (20 G) SHAVED PARMESAN CHEESE
½	CUP (10 G) PETITE GREENS

In a medium saucepan, bring 6 cups (1.4 L) water and the salt to a boil. Add the potatoes and cook until almost tender, about 6 minutes. Add the pole beans and cook until they're tender but still have a snap to them, about 3 minutes. Drain the potatoes and pole beans and transfer to an ice water bath. Remove from the ice water bath immediately after shocking. Spread the vegetables out on a kitchen towel to absorb the excess water. You do not want them wet when you mix the salad.

In a mixing bowl, toss the potatoes and pole beans, chile, and pickled onion with the vinaigrette. Transfer to a serving platter and top with the cheese and greens.

Lemon Herb Vinaigrette MAKES 2 CUPS (480 ML)

1	SHALLOT, *minced*
1	CLOVE GARLIC, *minced*
2	TABLESPOONS MINCED FRESH PARSLEY
½	TEASPOON MINCED FRESH THYME
½	TEASPOON SALT
¼	TEASPOON FRESHLY GROUND BLACK PEPPER
¼	TEASPOON GROUND CORIANDER
¼	CUP (60 ML) LEMON JUICE
¼	CUP (60 ML) CHAMPAGNE VINEGAR
¾	CUP (180 ML) OLIVE OIL
¾	CUP (180 ML) GRAPESEED OIL

In a bowl, combine the shallot, garlic, parsley, thyme, salt, pepper, and coriander. Stir and let sit for 5 minutes to macerate. Whisk in the lemon juice, vinegar, olive oil, and grapeseed oil. The dressing can be stored in the refrigerator for up to 1 week.

THE SOUTHERN COAST IS characterized by its sweltering summers, heavy with humidity. There is little refuge from the relentless heat. It is in this climate that the humble field peas thrive and have grown to become one of the South's most beloved vegetables. Fresh, plump pods come in a rainbow of colors during the summer: pink-eye peas, butter beans, crowder peas, lady peas, white acre peas . . . I could go on and on. My favorite pea is the zipper pea, retaining a splendid pop that gives way to a creamy interior when cooked. For this recipe, I reserve the coveted potlikker, the flavorful liquid the peas were cooked in, and turn it into a vinaigrette to dress the peas. If needed you can make this salad with dried black-eyed peas, which are the most common of all the field peas. Increase your cooking time if working with a dried pea.

Zipper Peas

with
Peaches and
Burrata

SERVES 4

3	TEASPOONS OLIVE OIL
1	MEDIUM SHALLOT, *finely diced*
2	CLOVES GARLIC, *minced*
1¼	POUNDS (570 G) SHELLED FRESH ZIPPER PEAS
1	BAY LEAF
2	TEASPOONS SALT
1	CUP (145 G) SMALL-DICE RED BELL PEPPER
1	TABLESPOON CHOPPED FRESH PARSLEY
1	TABLESPOON CHOPPED FRESH TARRAGON
½	CUP (120 ml) POTLIKKER VINAIGRETTE *(recipe follows)*
4	OUNCES (115 G) BURRATA CHEESE, *torn into bite-size pieces*
1	RIPE PEACH, *sliced into thin half-moons*
	SMALL BUNCH OF MICRO-BASIL, *or 6 basil leaves torn into pieces*

Potlikker Vinaigrette MAKES ¾ CUP (180 ML)

2	CUPS (480 ML) RESERVED POTLIKKER *(the cooking liquid from the peas)*
1	TEASPOON TABASCO SAUCE
2	TABLESPOONS CHAMPAGNE VINEGAR
1	TABLESPOON LEMON JUICE
¼	CUP (60 ML) OLIVE OIL
1½	TEASPOONS SALT

In a small saucepan over medium heat, bring the potlikker to a boil and reduce until only ½ cup (120 ml) remains. Let cool to room temperature. In a bowl, whisk together the reduced potlikker with the remaining ingredients. Taste for seasoning.

In a medium pot, heat 2 teaspoons of the oil over medium heat. Add the shallot and garlic and cook until soft, about 1 minute. Add the peas, bay leaf, salt, and 5 cups (1.2 L) water. Bring to a simmer and cook until the peas are tender but not mushy, 35 to 40 minutes. Let the peas cool in the liquid, then drain them, reserving 2 cups (480 ml) of the liquid for the vinaigrette.

While the peas are cooling, heat the remaining 1 teaspoon oil in a sauté pan over low heat. Add the bell pepper and cook gently until tender, about 6 minutes. Remove from the pan and let cool until ready to use.

In a mixing bowl, combine the zipper peas, bell pepper, parsley, tarragon, and vinaigrette.

Transfer to a serving dish and top with the burrata, peach, and basil. Serve immediately.

Chilled Pepper and Tomato Soup

SERVES 4
(7 CUPS/1.7 L)

THERE ARE DAYS WHEN it is too hot to cook. In fact, it's too hot to eat. The intense heat is inexplicably fatiguing, and when it's lunchtime, all I want is this cold, refreshing soup. Based on an Andalusian-style gazpacho, it is brightly acidic and makes perfect use of slightly overripe tomatoes. I prefer to pour this soup into a glass and drink it. Often when I make this, I bulk up the recipe to guarantee that there will be extra throughout the week.

2   POUNDS (910 G) HEIRLOOM RED OR YELLOW TOMATOES, *the riper the better*

1   SMALL CUCUMBER *(about 6 ounces/170 g)*

2   SMALL RED PEPPERS, *preferably something with a little spice to it, seeded*

1   SLICE OF BAGUETTE OR SIMILAR BREAD, *about 1 inch (2.5 cm) thick*

1   CLOVE GARLIC, *peeled*

1   TABLESPOON SALT

1   CUP (240 ML) GOOD-QUALITY EXTRA-VIRGIN OLIVE OIL, *plus more for garnish*

2   TABLESPOONS RED WINE VINEGAR

    ALEPPO CHILE

Cut the tomatoes in half. Using your fingers, scrape out the seeds over a bowl, catching any juice that spills out, and reserve.

Peel the cucumber and cut it in half lengthwise. Use a spoon to scrape out the seeds and discard. Roughly chop the tomatoes, cucumber, red peppers, garlic, and bread and place in a bowl.

Strain the reserved tomato juice to remove any seeds and add the liquid to the tomato-cucumber mixture. Add the salt and stir to combine. Let the mixture sit for 10 minutes to marinate.

Transfer to a blender with the oil and vinegar and blend on high speed until completely smooth. Check the seasoning and refrigerate until ready to serve. The colder it is, the better for a hot summer day. It can be stored in the refrigerator for up to 5 days.

To serve, garnish with olive oil and Aleppo chile.

IT'S EASY TO GO for what you know, but when it comes to produce, experiment! Italian eggplant is delicious, but there are more varieties waiting to be utilized. Fairytale eggplant is a petite variety, about 3 inches (7.5 cm) in length. It is a beautiful violet color with white speckles. They are hardy and resilient and grow well in the intense heat of summer. Fairytale eggplant are farmers' market staples, but harder to find at traditional grocery stores. However, you can substitute another small variety, like Japanese eggplant. For larger varieties, just increase the cooking time, tasting the eggplant to make sure it is tender and creamy and cooked through. The depth in this dish comes from the smoked tomato broth, which, when used as the braising liquid for the eggplants, reduces down into a rich and flavorful sauce.

Braised Fairytale Eggplant

in Smoky Tomato Broth

SERVES 2 AS A MAIN COURSE OR 4 AS A SIDE

1	TABLESPOON OLIVE OIL
8	OUNCES (225 G) FAIRYTALE EGGPLANT, *cut in half lengthwise and scored*
½	TEASPOON SALT
1	CUP (240 ML) SMOKY TOMATO BROTH *(recipe follows)*
1½	TABLESPOONS MINCED FRESH PARSLEY

Preheat the oven to 350°F (175°C).

In a large ovenproof sauté pan, heat the oil over medium-high heat. Add the eggplant, cut side down, and sear until golden brown, about 5 minutes. Flip the eggplant over and season with the salt. Add the broth, bring to a boil, and transfer the pan to the oven. Bake until the broth is reduced to a sauce consistency and coats the eggplant, about 15 minutes. Add the parsley and stir to combine. Serve immediately.

Smoky Tomato Broth MAKES 3 CUPS (720 ML)

1½	POUNDS (680 G) RIPE RED TOMATOES
1	TABLESPOON OLIVE OIL
½	ONION, *thinly sliced*
1	POBLANO PEPPER, *thinly sliced*
1	CLOVE GARLIC, *sliced*
1	TABLESPOON SMOKED PAPRIKA
1	TABLESPOON TOMATO PASTE
1	BAY LEAF
1	CUP (240 ML) DRY WHITE WINE
2	CUPS (480 ML) CHICKEN STOCK
1	TEASPOON SALT

Build a fire in a grill and let it burn down to medium heat (see Note).

Cut the tomatoes into quarters and place them on the grill grate. Cover the grill, making sure any air vents are closed, and cook the tomatoes until charred and soft, about 15 minutes.

Transfer the tomatoes to a blender and puree until smooth. You should have about 1½ cups (360 ml) puree. Set aside.

In a medium saucepan, heat the oil over medium-high heat. Add the onion, poblano, and garlic and cook until the vegetables are soft, about 3 minutes. Add the smoked paprika and cook for 1 minute. Add the tomato paste and bay leaf and cook for 1 minute. Deglaze the pan with the wine, bring to a boil, and reduce by half, about 4 minutes. Add the tomato puree, stock, and ½ cup (120 ml) water. Bring to a simmer and cook for 15 minutes. Stain the broth through a fine-mesh sieve into a bowl, discarding the solids, and season with the salt.

Extra broth can be frozen for up to 1 month.

NOTE *If you can't cook the tomatoes on a grill, you can use your oven. Toss the tomatoes in 2 tablespoons olive oil and roast them in a 425°F (205°C) oven for 15 to 20 minutes, until cooked through and lightly charred.*

Cantaloupe and Mouse Melons

with
Basil and Chile

SERVES 4 TO 6

MOUSE MELONS ARE A Cumberland Island colloquialism. More commonly known as Mexican sour gherkins, they are the size of small grapes and resemble watermelon. They retain a wonderful crisp crunch, even after being marinated, and taste like slightly sour cucumber. This salad came to life thanks to an overabundance from the garden. I was swimming in mouse melons and had several perfect cantaloupes. Thus, a dish was born. If you cannot find mouse melons, cucumbers cut into bite-size pieces make a great substitution.

3   CUPS (530 G) CANTALOUPE
    *scooped with a melon
    baller*

3   CUPS (315 G) MOUSE
    MELONS, *cut in half*

2   TEASPOONS OLIVE OIL

1   TEASPOON LIME JUICE

    PINCH OF SEA SALT

5   BASIL LEAVES, *torn*

½   TEASPOON ALEPPO CHILE

In a bowl, mix together the cantaloupe, mouse melons, oil, lime juice, and salt. Transfer to a serving dish and top with the basil and Aleppo chile. Serve immediately.

CHANTERELLES ARE A MARKER of summer in the South. While I enviously watch chefs from other regions flaunt their foraged mushrooms season after season, I wait for that small window of opportunity when a few wild chanterelles shyly emerge from the maritime forest floor, hidden under fallen oak leaves. Chanterelles have been increasingly easy to find at farmers' markets and grocery stores. If they're not available in your area, try maitake mushrooms as an alternative.

Grilled Skirt Steak

with Chanterelle Mushrooms and Romesco

SERVES 2

1¼ TEASPOONS SALT

½ TEASPOON FRESHLY GROUND BLACK PEPPER

½ TEASPOON SMOKED PAPRIKA

PINCH OF GARLIC POWDER

PINCH OF ONION POWDER

PINCH OF BROWN SUGAR

1 TEASPOON OLIVE OIL

1 (12-OUNCE/340 G) SKIRT STEAK, *trimmed*

1 TABLESPOON BUTTER

1 CLOVE GARLIC, *minced*

2 CUPS (140 G) CHANTERELLE MUSHROOMS *cut in half*

1 TEASPOON CHOPPED FRESH THYME

½ TEASPOON SHERRY VINEGAR

½ CUP (120 ML) ROMESCO *(recipe follows)*

HANDFUL OF ARUGULA

NOTE *If you can't cook on a grill, you can use your stove. Heat a large cast-iron pan over medium high. Add 1 tablespoon canola oil and sear the steak for 2 to 3 minutes on each side for medium-rare. Prepare the mushrooms in a medium sauté pan over medium heat.*

Romesco MAKES 1½ CUPS (360 ML)

2 RED BELL PEPPERS

2 TABLESPOONS OLIVE OIL

1 TOMATO, *cut into quarters*

2 CLOVES GARLIC, *peeled and smashed*

¼ TEASPOON ESPELETTE PEPPER

½ TEASPOON SMOKED PAPRIKA

1½ TEASPOON SALT

1 TEASPOON SHERRY VINEGAR

Build a fire in a grill and let it burn down to medium heat (see Note).

In a small bowl, mix together 1 teaspoon of the salt, the pepper, smoked paprika, garlic powder, onion powder, and brown sugar. Coat the steak with the oil and sprinkle both sides with the seasoning blend. Grill the steak for 2 to 3 minutes on each side for medium-rare. Transfer the steak to a platter and let rest for 5 minutes before slicing.

In a heavy cast-iron pan placed on the grill grates, melt the butter and add the garlic. Cook for 1 minute. Add the mushrooms and thyme and cook until the mushrooms are caramelized, about 5 minutes. Add the vinegar and remaining ¼ teaspoon salt. Stir to combine and remove the pan from the heat.

Spread the romesco on a platter. Slice the steak against the grain and place it on top of the romesco. Spoon the chanterelles over the steak and garnish the platter with arugula.

Preheat the oven to 350°F (175°C).

Roast the peppers over a direct flame on the stovetop until charred and blackened all over. (Alternatively, use your grill, if you have a fire lit and ready.) Transfer to a container, cover, and let the peppers steam.

Meanwhile, in a medium ovenproof sauté pan, heat the oil over medium-high heat. Add the tomato and transfer the pan to the oven and roast for 10 minutes. Remove the pan from the oven and flip the tomatoes over. Add the garlic cloves and return the pan to the oven. Cook until the garlic is golden brown, about 15 minutes. Remove the pan from the oven and stir in the Espelette pepper and smoked paprika. Set aside.

Peel the charred skin off the peppers and remove all the seeds from inside. Transfer the peppers to a blender and add the tomato mixture, scraping the pan to include all of the oil and caramelized bits. Add the salt and vinegar. Puree until smooth.

Romesco can be made ahead of time and stored in the refrigerator for up to 5 days. Bring to room temperature before serving.

Watermelon Juice

MAKES 4 CUPS (960 ML)

THERE ARE DEFINING MOMENTS in all of our childhoods in which food can take on legendary status. The first time I had watermelon juice, I was transfixed. Possibly because it was the first time I had ever had a glass of juice made from all fresh ingredients. There was a luxury to that moment that I still associate with a glass of watermelon juice. Luckily for me, watermelons are held in high regard during summers in the South. When working watermelon onto a menu, I always save the scraps to blend up this drink.

2½ POUNDS (1.2 KG) CHOPPED
    SEEDLESS WATERMELON

2   TABLESPOONS LIME JUICE

1   TABLESPOON HONEY

    PINCH OF SALT

In a blender, combine all of the ingredients and puree until smooth. Strain through a fine-mesh sieve into a pitcher. The juice can be stored in the refrigerator for up to 5 days.

The Lure of the
SURF AND
THE SEA

As the heat of summer intensifies, so does the need to seek out the ocean. I learned to surf (take that word lightly) in the warm waters of the Atlantic. It is fairly comical considering I grew up in California. But it is in these messy, little, inconsistent waves that I find comfort. For someone who has spent the majority of their working career in a professional kitchen, stress and tension are a lifestyle. But the ocean is the one place where my focus cannot be the count for the night, the prep of the day, or the event two weeks out. The focus has to be on the waves. However small they can look from the beach, meeting a wave face to face when lying flat on a surfboard will command your attention. Stripped down, immersed in the sea, we are completely vulnerable. The ocean will punch you, roll you up, and spit you out. Saltwater will burn your eyes, and mottled little bruises will be worn like badges of honor. But for those moments of battle you will be rewarded. The exhilaration of catching one wave will cling to your memory, luring you back. There is a particular feeling after surfing that can only be understood from experience, a mix of being refreshingly exhausted and replenished—a feeling that is the particular gift that only saltwater can offer.

Pan-Roasted Vermillion Snapper

with Tomato Jam and Coconut Broth

SERVES 4

THERE ARE NIGHTS DURING the summer when the wind brushes the oleander in such a way that I swear I live on a Caribbean island. The banana trees, lemongrass, and ginger that proliferate here help to perpetuate this feeling. Inspired by my tropical surroundings, this dish has a complex layering of flavors using spices and herbs. The aromatic coconut broth is spiked with lemongrass, ginger, cilantro, and chiles. The tomato jam is given extra depth with the use of berbere spice, an Ethiopian spice blend that incorporates fenugreek, coriander, and allspice. A little extra sprinkle of this versatile spice on the seared fish rounds out this satisfying dish.

4	(5-OUNCE/140 G) PORTIONS OF VERMILLION SNAPPER FILLET, *skin removed*
2	TEASPOONS SALT
1	TEASPOON BERBERE SPICE BLEND
2	TABLESPOONS CANOLA OIL
1	TABLESPOON BUTTER
1	TABLESPOON LIME JUICE
1	TABLESPOON MINCED CILANTRO
1	CUP (240 ML) TOMATO JAM *(recipe follows)*
1	CUP (240 ML) COCONUT BROTH *(recipe follows)*
4	BASIL LEAVES

Season the snapper with the salt and berbere.

In a large sauté pan or heavy cast-iron pan, heat the oil over medium-high heat until very hot. Add the snapper fillets and cook until the edges are golden brown, about 3 minutes. Reduce the heat to medium-low and add the butter. Cook for an additional 20 seconds, then flip the fish over and add the lime juice. Carefully tilt the pan toward you and use a large spoon to baste the fish with the hot butter and lime juice; continue basting until the fish is cooked through, about 2 minutes. Remove the fish from the pan and set aside on a warm plate until ready to serve.

Divide the jam among four large entrée bowls. Add ¼ cup (60 ml) broth to each and place a portion of fish next to the tomato jam. Garnish each bowl with a basil leaf and serve.

Tomato Jam MAKES 1 CUP (240 ML)

1	TEASPOON COCONUT OIL
1	TEASPOON BERBERE SPICE BLEND
1	SHALLOT, *finely diced*
1	CLOVE GARLIC, *minced*
½	SERRANO CHILE, *seeded and finely diced*
2	TEASPOONS PEELED AND MINCED FRESH GINGER
2	CUPS (360 G) SMALL-DICE TOMATOES
1	TABLESPOON TOMATO PASTE
1	TEASPOON SALT
1½	TABLESPOONS MINCED FRESH CILANTRO

In a small saucepan, heat the coconut oil over medium-low heat. Add the berbere, shallot, garlic, chile, and ginger and cook until softened, about 5 minutes. Add the tomatoes, tomato paste, and salt and cook, stirring occasionally, until the mixture is thickened and jam-like, about 18 minutes. Remove from the heat and stir in the cilantro. Keep warm until ready to serve. The jam can be made ahead and stored in the refrigerator for up to 5 days. Warm before serving.

Coconut Broth MAKES 1 CUP (240 ML)

- 1 TEASPOON COCONUT OIL
- 1 SHALLOT, *thinly sliced*
- 1 TABLESPOON PEELED AND CHOPPED FRESH GINGER
- ½ SERRANO CHILE, *thinly sliced*
- 1 LEMONGRASS STALK, *thinly sliced*
- 1 CLOVE GARLIC, *sliced*
- ½ TEASPOON BROWN SUGAR
- ¼ TEASPOON FISH SAUCE
- ½ CUP (120 ML) CLAM JUICE *(bottled)*
- 1 CUP (240 ML) COCONUT MILK
- 2 SPRIGS OF CILANTRO
- 1 TEASPOON LIME JUICE
- ½ TEASPOON SALT

In a small saucepan, heat the coconut oil over medium heat. Add the shallot, ginger, chile, lemongrass, and garlic and cook until lightly caramelized, about 4 minutes. Add the brown sugar and fish sauce and stir to combine. Add the clam juice, coconut milk, and cilantro and bring to a simmer; reduce for 5 minutes. Strain the broth through a fine-mesh sieve into a bowl and stir in the lime juice and salt. Keep warm until ready to serve.

The broth can be made ahead and stored in the refrigerator for up to 5 days. Warm before serving.

LEARN TO DEBONE A chicken thigh, and you will never want to cook a chicken breast again. It is a very simple process and it's more intuitive than anything else. Make sure to buy chicken thighs with skin on them! Once the thigh is deboned, the trick is to cook it low and slow so that the skin crisps up. Letting the fat render out will result in a lacquered chicken thigh with a potato chip–style crunch. Look for a dark golden-brown sear.

Crispy Chicken Thighs

with Smoked Eggplant

SERVES 2

2	TEASPOONS SALT
1	TEASPOON PAPRIKA
2	TEASPOON ZA'ATAR SPICE BLEND
4	CHICKEN THIGHS, DEBONED *(see Note)*
1	TABLESPOON OLIVE OIL
4	THIN SLICES LEMON
1½	CUPS (360 ML) SMOKED EGGPLANT PUREE *(recipe follows)*

Combine the salt, paprika, and za'atar. Using all of the salt mixture, season both sides of the chicken thighs.

Heat the oil in a large sauté pan over medium-low heat. When the oil is hot, add the chicken, skin side down. Use a spatula to gently press down and flatten the thighs every few minutes to ensure contact with the pan. Cook for 15 to 20 minutes, adjusting the heat between low and medium-low heat, until the skin is crispy and golden brown. Lay the lemon slices in the pan next to the thighs. Cook for 1 minute. Flip the thighs over and cook until the chicken is cooked through, about 3 minutes.

Remove the chicken from the pan and allow to rest skin side up until ready to serve. Serve with the eggplant puree.

NOTE *Deboning chicken thighs is easier than you might think—there is just one bone to take out. I recommend using a boning knife if you have one; if not, use the sharpest knife you have. Lay the thigh skin side down on a cutting board. Take your knife and make an incision on both sides of the bone. Use your fingers to separate the bone from the meat. Turn the knife horizontally and cut along the underside of the bone, away from you. Spin the thigh around and repeat the process to cut out the bone.*

Smoked Eggplant Puree MAKES 1½ CUPS (360 ML)

1	LARGE EGGPLANT (ABOUT 12 OUNCES/340 G)
2	CLOVES GARLIC, PEELED
1	TEASPOON PLUS 1 TABLESPOON OLIVE OIL
1	TABLESPOON PLAIN YOGURT
1	TEASPOON LEMON JUICE
1¼	TEASPOONS SALT, *or more to taste*
¼	TEASPOON CAYENNE POWDER
¼	TEASPOON GROUND CUMIN
¼	TEASPOON GROUND CORIANDER

Build a fire in a grill and let it burn down to medium heat (see Note).

Put the eggplant on the grill grate and cook, covered, turning as needed, until well charred and very soft inside, about 25 minutes. Let cool slightly, so it is not too hot to handle.

While the eggplant is roasting, put the garlic cloves and 1 teaspoon of the oil in a small piece of aluminum foil, folding the edges to make a package. Place on the grill grate and roast until tender, about 15 minutes.

Cut open and scoop out all of the flesh of the eggplant, avoiding the charred skin, and transfer to a food processor along with the roasted garlic and its oil. Add the remaining ingredients and puree until smooth. Season to taste as needed and serve warm.

The puree can be stored in the refrigerator for up to 5 days. Warm before serving.

NOTE *If you can't cook the eggplant on a grill, you can use your oven. Preheat the oven to 400°F (205°C). Place the eggplant on a baking sheet and cook until the eggplant is very soft inside, about 40 minutes. Let cool slightly, so it is not too hot to handle. While the eggplant is roasting, put the garlic cloves and 1 teaspoon oil in a small piece of aluminum foil, folding the edges to make a package. Add to the oven and roast until tender, about 15 minutes.*

The Case for
SPICES

Spice is often misunderstood. It does not mean imminent heat or overpowering flavor. Defined as *an aromatic or pungent seed, fruit, root, bark, or other vegetable substance used to flavor food*, spices are the foundation of my cooking.

Spices can be one individual product like cumin or it can be a blend like za'atar. Blends often offer an opportunity to taste from a specific region in the world. They also take the guesswork out of how to match flavors. Spice blends will vary in strength and types of spices used, depending on whose making it, so try different producers.

One of your first choices will be whether to buy whole or ground. If you are just starting your spice collection and are looking for ease, opt for ground. Whole spices require a spice grinder (or a sturdy coffee grinder) but can guarantee freshness. Many spices contain oils that are essential to their flavor. When a spice is ground, the oils are released and the spice will begin to lose its pungency. Therefore, ground spices start off at a disadvantage to their whole counterparts. Spices are best when fresh, having more aromas and flavor. If you have a jar of paprika from two years ago, throw it out. Taste your spices; if you taste nothing or just a very dull flavor, it's old and time to replace it.

Learning to work with spices will change your cooking. With spice, you need less fat, which means healthier meals. It has taken me years of study to learn about spices, and I still have so much more to learn. Come summer and early fall, herbs wilt in the intense heat but my spice shelf stays stocked. Check out page 35 for more information on where to buy spices.

Here are some favorite spices I like to keep on hand . . .

ALEPPO CHILE—Mild, pleasant heat with fruity flavor and slight salinity

BENNE SEED—Rich, nutty flavor

DRIED HIBISCUS FLOWERS—Tart, acidic flavor with light floral notes

CALABRIAN CHILES—Dried or packed in oil, salty, and flavorful with medium-high heat

CAYENNE—Tart and spicy with a clean straightforward heat

CELERY SEED—Aromatic with notes of citrus and parsley, strong savory flavor

CHINESE FIVE SPICE—Commonly used in Chinese cooking, this spice blend balances the flavors of sweet, sour, bitter, heat, and salt with the use of star anise, clove, pepper, cinnamon, and fennel

CORIANDER—Fruity aromas with a warm and nutty flavor

CUMIN—Earthy scent with a sharp and slightly bitter flavor

ESPELETTE PEPPER—Robust and smoky with a mild fruity heat

FENNEL SEEDS—Mild anise flavor with sweet and savory notes

GROUND GINGER—Pungent and bright with citrus and spicy flavors

GUAJILLO CHILES—Mild heat with a sweet raisin flavor

HUNGARIAN PAPRIKA—Mild and slightly sweet, imparting a red color

PIMENTÓN DE LA VERA DULCE—Gently smoked chiles from Spain with a sweet, smoky flavor

SAFFRON—Distinct flavor and strong fragrance with floral and honey notes

SUMAC—Tart and sour flavor

TURMERIC—Peppery and warm, imparting its distinct golden color

VIETNAMESE CINNAMON—Warm and woody spice, highly aromatic

SPICE BLENDS

BERBERE—Ethiopian spice blend with earthy flavors of chile and fenugreek

HARISSA—North African condiment and dried spice blend made with dried chile, garlic, and coriander

HERBES DE PROVENCE—From the South of France, a blend of rosemary, marjoram, tarragon, oregano, and lavender

RAS EL HANOUT—"The Jewel of the Shop," a North African spice blend that contain up to forty different spices, often with notes of cinnamon, cumin, coriander, and various peppers

SHICHIMI TOGARASHI—Japanese spice blend made with dried chiles, sansho pepper, and citrus

VADOUVAN—French for sundried spices, a blend of dried onion, shallots, and garlic with curry spice

ZA'ATAR—Middle Eastern blend made with oregano, thyme, and sesame seeds

Southern Rice Bowl

of Okra,
Eggplant,
Chanterelles, and
Lemongrass

SERVES 4

LEMONGRASS GROWS WELL IN our semitropical climate. It's an herb that lends itself to building subtle citrus flavor without adding acidity. Paired with ginger, it pleasantly contrasts with spicy foods. The intention of this dish is to showcase these aromatic, complex flavors while highlighting southern ingredients during their peak season. While you can work in new vegetables as the seasons change, this is my all-time favorite combination.

4	TABLESPOONS (60 ML) OLIVE OIL
2	CUPS (190 G) DICED EGGPLANT
2	CUPS (200 G) THINLY SLICED OKRA
2	CUPS (140 G) CHANTERELLE MUSHROOMS, *cleaned and cut in half*
1½	TEASPOONS SALT
4	CUPS (630 G) COOKED CAROLINA GOLD RICE *(recipe follows)*
4	CUPS (960 ML) LEMONGRASS BROTH *(recipe follows)*
	SMALL BUNCH OF BASIL

In a large sauté pan or heavy cast-iron pan, heat 3 tablespoons of the oil over medium-high heat. Add the eggplant and cook, stirring often, until caramelized and tender, about 8 minutes. Remove the eggplant from the pan and set aside. In the same pan, heat the remaining 1 tablespoon oil over medium-high heat. Add the okra and cook until slightly charred, about 5 minutes. Add the mushrooms and cook until slightly caramelized, about 5 minutes. Remove from the heat and stir in the eggplant and salt.

Divide the rice among four serving bowls. Ladle in 1 cup of the broth per bowl. Equally divide the vegetables among the bowls and garnish with basil. Serve immediately.

Carolina Gold Rice MAKES 4 CUPS (630 G)

1½	CUPS (275 G) CAROLINA GOLD RICE
1	TABLESPOON OLIVE OIL
1	TEASPOON SALT
1	BAY LEAF

Put the rice in a bowl, cover with cold water, and stir with your hand. The water will turn cloudy from the starch in the rice. Drain the rice in a fine-mesh sieve and return it to the bowl.

Repeat this process until the water becomes fairly clear, about five passes. Let the rice drain in the sieve and set aside.

In a small saucepan, bring 2¼ cups (540 ml) water, the oil, salt, and bay leaf to a boil. Add the rice and stir once. Bring back to a boil. Cover the pan and reduce the heat to low. Cook for 15 minutes. Remove from the heat and let stand, covered, for 5 minutes. Remove the lid and fluff the rice with a fork.

Keep warm until ready to serve.

Lemongrass Broth MAKES 5 CUPS (1.2 L)

1	TEASPOON OLIVE OIL
2	STALKS LEMONGRASS, *thinly sliced (about 1 cup)*
1	(1-INCH/2.5 CM) PIECE FRESH GINGER, *peeled and thinly sliced*
1	JALAPEÑO, *seeded and sliced*
1	SHALLOT, *sliced*
1	CLOVE GARLIC, *sliced*
1	TEASPOON WHOLE CORIANDER SEEDS
	SMALL HANDFUL OF CILANTRO SPRIGS
4	CUPS (960 ML) CHICKEN STOCK
2	TEASPOONS SALT

In a medium saucepan, heat the oil over medium heat. Add the lemongrass, ginger, jalapeño, shallot, garlic, and coriander seeds. Cook until lightly caramelized, about 4 minutes. Add the cilantro, stock, and 2 cups (480 ml) water. Bring to a boil, then lower the heat to a gentle simmer and cook until slightly reduced, about 25 minutes. Stir in the salt and strain the broth through a fine-mesh sieve into a bowl and discard the solids.

Keep warm until ready to use. The broth can be made ahead and stored for up to 5 days in the refrigerator or frozen for up to 1 month. Warm before serving.

THIS DISH IS LEGENDARY in the kitchens I've cooked in. It can convert even the rare but fervent corn cynic. The sweet summer corn is lightly charred and slowly simmered in a rich corn-infused cream and topped with shrimp that is gently poached in butter. I like to finish this dish with a little heat provided by the smoked serrano chile flakes, but you can keep it mild by using sweet paprika.

Cast-Iron Sweet Corn and Buttered Shrimp

SERVES 6

10	EARS OF CORN, *shucked*
2	TABLESPOONS PLUS 1 CUP (2 STICKS/255 G) BUTTER
½	CUP (70 G) MINCED ONION
½	CUP (120 ML) HEAVY CREAM
2½	TEASPOONS SALT
1	POUND (455 G) SHRIMP, *peeled and deveined*
3	TABLESPOONS WHITE WINE
1	BAY LEAF
1	TEASPOON SMOKED SERRANO CHILI FLAKES
1	TABLESPOON MINCED FRESH CILANTRO

Remove the corn kernels from the cobs by standing the ears up over a wide baking dish and carefully cutting down the sides of the corn with a sharp knife. Then hold the corncob over a bowl and use the flat side of a butter knife to scrape down on the cob to extract the "milk." Reserve the corn "milk" and discard the scraped cobs.

In a large cast-iron pan, heat 2 tablespoons of the butter over medium-high heat. Add the corn kernels and onion and cook, stirring occasionally, until the corn becomes slightly charred, about 7 minutes. Add the cream and reserved corn milk and reduce for 1 to 2 minutes. Stir in 2 teaspoons of the salt and remove from the heat. Set aside and keep warm.

Cut the shrimp into small bite-size pieces and set aside.

In a small saucepan over low heat, add the wine, the remaining ½ teaspoon salt, and the remaining 1 cup (2 sticks/255 g) butter. Bring to a simmer. Add the shrimp and bay leaf and gently poach until the shrimp is cooked through, about 5 minutes. Remove the shrimp from the butter with a slotted spoon.

Transfer the corn to a serving dish and top with the butter-poached shrimp. Garnish with the smoked chile flakes and cilantro and serve immediately.

What to do with
PEPPERS

Peppers thrive in the long, hot summer of the southeast coast. From regional favorites like datil peppers to ubiquitous jalapeños, an excess of summer peppers offers an opportunity for preservation. Here are two of my favorite ways to work through an excess of peppers.

SPICES

Make your own paprika, cayenne, or serrano chile flakes. Whatever kind of pepper you have, turn it into a spice. Smoking is optional to impart flavor.

1. Clean your peppers. Cut in half, and then seed them.

2. Smoke on a grill over indirect heat, covered. This is only to impart smoke, not to cook the peppers (30 minutes should do the trick).

3. Use a dehydrator to dry the peppers; they will easily snap in half when done.

4. Grind in a spice grinder or coffee grinder to desired size. Store in an airtight container for up to 6 months.

HOT SAUCE

Jalapeños turn bright red when left on the vine and make a pleasantly spicy hot sauce. The heat of your hot sauce will vary depending on the heat of your pepper.

1. Clean your peppers. Make sure there are no blemishes or holes.

2. Roughly chop the peppers, seeds and all. Discard the stems.

3. Mix the peppers and salt: A ratio of 2 pounds (910 g) chopped peppers to ½ pound (225 g) salt is a good start. Place in a container with an airtight lid and let sit at room temperature for 4 days.

4. Rinse the salt off the peppers and let drain.

5. Put the peppers in a medium pot and cover by 2 inches (5 cm) with a mixture of equal parts distilled white vinegar and water. Bring to a simmer and cook for 10 minutes.

6. Transfer to a blender and puree. Store in an airtight container in the refrigerator for up to 3 months.

Watermelon Granita

SERVES 8

COLD, SLUSHY SPOONFULS OF watermelon granita are a preferred method of cooling down on an intensely humid day. Watermelon is a popular fruit on the southeast coast, but the inspiration for this treat comes straight from my childhood imagination. To the best of my knowledge, every grade school has an underground candy smuggling ring. In my grade school, the candy of choice was Vero Rebanaditas. These Mexican candies are watermelon-flavored lollipops covered with chile powder, lime, and salt. This recipe pays tributes to these intensely flavorful little candies.

2   POUNDS (910 G) CHOPPED SEEDLESS WATERMELON

6   TABLESPOONS (75 G) SUGAR

6   TABLESPOONS (90 ML) LIME JUICE

½   TEASPOON SPICY CHILE FLAKES, *such as arbol or cayenne, plus more for serving, if desired*

¼   TEASPOON SALT

Put all the ingredients in a blender and puree until smooth. Strain the puree through a fine-mesh sieve into a wide baking dish. Discard the solids.

Place the watermelon juice in the freezer and scrape using a fork every 25 minutes or so until the juice has crystallized and looks like shaved ice, 2 to 3 hours.

To serve, scoop granita into chilled bowls. Garnish with a little extra chile if you like spice!

The granita can be made a few days ahead and kept in the freezer covered or wrapped in plastic. Scrape with a fork again before serving.

IT'S HARD TO IGNORE peach season in the South. Finding the perfect peach is a rite of passage. While peach trees do not grow particularly well on the coast, we are surrounded by them with Georgia and South Carolina boasting roadside stands selling this iconic southern fruit. Cooking peaches only helps to intensify their floral sweetness. While the batter bakes, the sugar, butter, and fruit caramelize at the bottom and soak into what will become the top layer of the cake. When you flip the cake (the most daunting of moments), the lovely sweet perfumed scent of roasted peaches will be released, and an amber-hued sauce will pool at the bottom of your cake. I like to pair this with whipped sour cream and a cup of black coffee.

Peach Upside-Down Cake

with Whipped Sour Cream

MAKES
1 (9-INCH/
23 CM) CAKE

½ CUP (1 STICK/115 G) PLUS 7 TABLESPOONS (100 G) BUTTER, *at room temperature*

1 CUP (220 G) BROWN SUGAR

2 TABLESPOONS BOURBON WHISKEY

½ TEASPOON GROUND CINNAMON

PINCH OF SEA SALT

2 LARGE RIPE PEACHES, *pitted and thinly sliced*

1½ CUPS (190 G) ALL-PURPOSE FLOUR

1½ TEASPOONS BAKING POWDER

½ TEASPOON KOSHER SALT

1 CUP (200 G) GRANULATED SUGAR

3 LARGE EGGS

2 TEASPOONS VANILLA EXTRACT

¾ CUP (180 ML) BUTTERMILK

3 CUPS (720 ML) WHIPPED SOUR CREAM *(recipe follows)*

Preheat the oven to 350°F (175°C). Grease a 9-inch (23 cm) round cake pan with 1 tablespoon of the butter and line the bottom with parchment paper.

In a small pot, melt 6 tablespoons (85 g) of the butter with the brown sugar, Bourbon, cinnamon, and sea salt over medium heat. Stir to combine. Pour the mixture into the prepared cake pan and spread evenly on the bottom. Layer in the peach slices, starting in the center and working outward to form a spiral shape that covers the bottom of the pan. Set aside while you make the batter.

In a small bowl, sift together the flour and baking powder. Stir in the kosher salt. Set aside.

In an electric mixer, use a paddle attachment to beat the remaining ½ cup (115 g) butter with the granulated sugar on medium speed until light and airy, about 3 minutes. Beat in the eggs one at a time, stopping to scrape the bottom of the bowl between each addition. Add in the vanilla. With the mixer running on medium-low speed, in three passes, add in the flour mixture and buttermilk, alternating between the two. Mix until incorporated.

Spread the batter into the cake pan over the peach slices. Bake until the top is golden brown and a tester inserted in center comes out clean, about 40 minutes. Allow the cake to cool at room temperature for about 15 minutes. Run a butter knife around the inside edge of the pan to make sure the cake is not sticking and invert the cake onto a platter to release it from the pan.

Serve slightly warm with the whipped sour cream on the side.

Whipped Sour Cream MAKES 3 CUPS (720 ML)

1½ CUPS (360 ML) HEAVY CREAM

3 TABLESPOONS SOUR CREAM

3 TABLESPOONS CONFECTIONERS' SUGAR

In an electric mixer, use a whisk attachment to combine the cream, sour cream, and confectioners' sugar. Mix on high speed until medium peaks form. (Alternatively, whisk by hand and get a good workout.) Refrigerate until ready to use. It can be stored in the refrigerator for up to 5 days.

HOW TO

FRY A FISH

SALTWATER TRADITIONS

Fishing is a family tradition on the south-east coast. Come summertime, it is hard to find a creek, dock, or river that doesn't have a fishing pole cast out in it. A favored way to cook the prize of the day is a fish fry. Pile a table full of perfectly fried local catch, platters of fat summer tomatoes, marinated field peas, crispy cucumber slaw, and tartar sauce spiked with chow-chow (a tasty Southern pickled relish) for the makings of an iconic Southern meal.

OUTDOORS IS BEST

During the peak of summer this is a meal that will lure you out from the safety of the air-conditioning. Invite too many people, make sure there are pets and kids running around in the yard, and have a weathered table stacked high with lemon wedges, hot sauce, and beverages perspiring in the heat. You can fry fish in your house, but be warned, your house will smell like a fish camp for twenty-four to forty-eight hours afterward.

PLAN AHEAD

Dredge your fish ahead of time. A good dredge makes for a good fry. A fish can be dredged a few hours in advance of cooking and kept in the fridge. When cooking outdoors, use an outdoor burner with a propane tank. Fill your pot wisely. Make sure your pot is large enough to hold the oil and the fish that will displace the oil. A large pot only needs to be half full. Set yourself up with a wire rack on a baking pan, or a large plate lined with paper towels, and a spider or slotted spoon for lowering and lifting your fish in and out of the oil. Be ready with this before you drop your first piece of fish in the oil.

FRY LIKE A PRO

Don't put too many pieces of fish into the oil at the same time. It will drop your oil temperature. Let the oil reheat to frying temperature before you add the next batch of fish to the oil. When you are done, turn off the heat under the oil, cover the pot, and let it cool before you clean up. If you have another fish fry in your future, strain any fried bits out of the oil and reserve the oil for future use.

SUMMER FISH FRY

Cornmeal-Dusted Fried Flounder, White Acre Peas with Cherry Tomatoes, Cucumber Slaw, Chowchow Tartar Sauce SERVES 6

Cornmeal-Dusted Fried Flounder

2	QUARTS (2 L) CANOLA OIL
6	(4-OUNCE/115 G) PORTIONS OF FOUNDER FILLET
2½	TEASPOONS SALT
½	CUP (50 G) UNSEASONED BREADCRUMBS
½	CUP (65 G) ALL-PURPOSE FLOUR
½	CUP (90 G) FINELY GROUND CORNMEAL
1	TEASPOON ONION POWDER
1	TEASPOON GARLIC POWDER
1	TEASPOON SMOKED PAPRIKA
1	TEASPOON CAYENNE POWDER
½	CUP (120 ML) BUTTERMILK
1	TEASPOON HOT SAUCE

In a large 4-quart (3.8 L) pot, heat the oil to 350°F (175°C). Season the fish with 1 teaspoon of the salt. In a bowl, whisk together the breadcrumbs, flour, cornmeal, onion powder, garlic powder, smoked paprika, cayenne, and remaining 1½ teaspoons salt.

In another bowl, whisk together the buttermilk and hot sauce. Add the fish to the buttermilk mixture and toss to combine. Take one portion of the fish and transfer it to the seasoned flour mixture and toss to evenly coat it. Transfer the dredged fish to a wire rack until ready to fry. Repeat with the remaining fish.

Working in batches, two pieces at a time, lower the fish into the fry oil and cook until golden brown and the bubbles have subsided, about 4 to 5 minutes. Transfer the fish to a wire rack.

White Acre Peas with Cherry Tomatoes

1	CUP (145 G) CHERRY TOMATOES, cut in half
	PINCH OF SEA SALT
½	CUP (120 ML) LEMON HERB VINAIGRETTE (page 194)
4	CUPS (630 G) COOKED WHITE ACRE PEAS, or other field pea variety (see cooking method on page 197)
1	TEASPOON CHOPPED FRESH PARSLEY
	KOSHER SALT

Toss the tomatoes with the sea salt and about 2 tablespoons of the vinaigrette. Combine the peas with the remaining vinaigrette, the parsley, and kosher salt. Top with the cherry tomatoes.

Cucumber Slaw

1	POUND (455 G) CUCUMBERS, cut in half lengthwise and thinly sliced
1	RED BELL PEPPER, cut in half lengthwise and thinly sliced
¼	RED ONION, thinly sliced
¼	HEAD GREEN CABBAGE, thinly sliced
2	TEASPOONS CHOPPED FRESH PARSLEY
1	TEASPOON CHOPPED FRESH MINT
1	TEASPOON HONEY
1½	TABLESPOONS CIDER VINEGAR
2	TABLESPOONS OLIVE OIL
¾	TEASPOON SALT

Combine all the ingredients together in a bowl and mix well. Slaw can be made several hours ahead and kept in the refrigerator until ready to serve.

Chowchow Tartar Sauce MAKES 1 CUP (240 ML)

¼	CUP (60 ML) DRAINED CHOWCHOW
¾	CUP (180 ML) MAYONNAISE
¼	TEASPOON MINCED FRESH DILL
¼	TEASPOON MINCED FRESH PARSLEY
½	TEASPOON WORCESTERSHIRE SAUCE
½	TEASPOON TABASCO SAUCE
	PINCH OF SALT

Combine all of the ingredients and mix well. The sauce can be made ahead and stored in the refrigerator for up to 5 days.

FALL IS A TIME of transition. The hot and humid weather breaks as hurricanes swell and threaten. A collective sigh of relief arrives with the end of storm season and cooler temperatures are welcomed like an old friend. Downed oak and cedar trees from storms past are gathered and cured for fires to be built in the coming winter. The golden light of fall draws us outdoors.

The acorns begin to drop and crunch underfoot while turkeys can be seen rooting around in the early morning mist. Instinctively my cooking begins to take on more richness. Root vegetables and winter squash come back to the table. Slow cooking and wood grilling are reasons to linger a little longer over the warmth of a fire.

SMOKE & CEDAR

SEASON

OCTOBER–DECEMBER

GRILLED HEAD-ON SHRIMP TOSSED IN CAPER GREMOLATA

CAST-IRON FLATBREAD

GRILLED LETTUCE WITH HERBED YOGURT DRESSING

SLOW-ROASTED FALL TOMATOES

GARLIC CONFIT

ALSO PICTURED: WHITE ACRE PEAS WITH CHERRY TOMATOES (PAGE 228) AND CAST-IRON FILET BEANS TOSSED IN PIPERADE AND BENNE SEED (PAGE 157)

GRILLED HEAD-ON SHRIMP

SERVES 6

- 3 POUNDS (1.4 KG) HEAD-ON
     SHRIMP (see Notes)
- 3 TABLESPOONS OLIVE OIL

     CRUNCHY CAPER GREMOLATA
     (recipe follows)

Build a fire in a grill and let it burn down to
medium heat (see Notes).

Dab the excess moisture from the shrimp. In
a bowl, toss the shrimp with the oil. Make sure
the shrimp are evenly coated. Place the shrimp on
the grill grate in a single layer. Cook until bright
pink and lightly charred, about 3 minutes. Flip the
shrimp using tongs, and cook the other side until
bright pink and the tails are tightly curled, about
3 minutes. Remove the shrimp from the grill and
place in a bowl. Toss with the gremolata and serve.

NOTES *If head-on shrimp aren't available, use
6 ounces (170 g) headless shrimp per person.*

*If you can't cook the shrimp on a grill, you
can use your oven. Preheat the broiler on high.
Arrange the oil coated shrimp on a sheet pan in
a single layer and place about 8 inches under the
broiler. Cook until bright pink and lightly charred,
about 3 minutes. Flip the shrimp using tongs and
cook the other side until bright pink and tails are
tightly curled, about 3 minutes. Remove the shrimp
from the broiler and place in a bowl. Toss with the
gremolata and serve.*

CRUNCHY CAPER GREMOLATA

MAKES 1 CUP (240 ML)

- 2   CUPS (480 ML) CANOLA OIL
- 1   CUP (140 G) DRAINED
       CAPERS, *patted dry*
- ¼   CUP (13 G) FINELY CHOPPED
       FRESH PARSLEY
- ¾   CUP (180 ML) OLIVE OIL
       ZEST OF 1 LEMON
- 1   TEASPOON ALEPPO CHILE
- ½   TEASPOON HONEY

In a small pot, heat the canola oil over medium
heat. When the oil reaches 325°F (165°C), carefully
add half of the capers. Cook until the bubbles have
subsided and the capers have burst open, about
1½ minutes. Remove the capers with a slotted
spoon and place on a plate lined with a paper towel.
Repeat the process with the remaining capers.

In a bowl, combine the parsley, olive oil, lemon
zest, Aleppo chile, and honey. Stir in the fried capers
and serve immediately.

CAST-IRON FLATBREAD

MAKES 8 (2¾-OUNCE/75 G) PORTIONS

     FLATBREAD DOUGH (PAGE 48)
- 4 TABLESPOONS (60 ML) OLIVE
     OIL

Prepare the flatbread dough as described on
page 48.

Roll out each portion of dough into a 4-inch
(10 cm) round, about ¼ inch (6 mm) thick. Liberally flour your surface and rolling pin so the dough
will not stick.

In a large cast-iron pan, heat ½ tablespoon of
olive oil over medium-high heat. When the oil is
hot, gently place one dough round flat into the pan.
Cook for 1 to 2 minutes, or until dough begins to
gently brown and bubbles begin to appear. Flip
dough and cook for an additional minute. Remove
flatbread from pan and keep warm. Repeat process
with remaining dough rounds.

GRILLED LETTUCE WITH HERBED YOGURT DRESSING

SERVES 6

¾   CUP (180 ML) PLAIN YOGURT

1   TABLESPOON MINCED FRESH
    DILL

1   TABLESPOON MINCED FRESH
    CHIVES

1   TABLESPOON MINCED FRESH
    PARSLEY

¾   TEASPOON SALT

¼   TEASPOON LEMON JUICE

3   HEARTS OF ROMAINE LETTUCE

3   TEASPOONS OLIVE OIL

To make the dressing, in a small bowl, combine the yogurt, dill, chives, parsley, ½ teaspoon of the salt, the lemon juice, and 2 tablespoons water. Keep in the refrigerator until ready to serve.

Build a fire in a grill and let it burn down to high heat (see Note).

Prepare the romaine hearts by cutting them in half and washing them. Dry completely. Brush the cut romaine with the oil and season with the remaining ¼ teaspoon salt. Place the romaine, cut side down, on the grill. Cook until the leaves are lightly charred, about 2 minutes. Flip and sear on opposite side for 1 minute. Remove from the heat.

Spread the yogurt dressing on the base of a plate. Place the grilled romaine hearts on top. Drizzle with a little more yogurt dressing and serve immediately.

NOTE *If you can't cook the lettuce on a grill, you can use your oven. Prepare the romaine hearts by cutting them in half and washing them. Dry completely. Brush the cut romaine with the oil and season with the remaining ¼ teaspoon salt. Heat a cast-iron pan over high heat. Sear the romaine, cut side down, until lightly charred, about 2 minutes. Flip and sear lightly on the opposite side for 1 minute. Remove from heat.*

SLOW-ROASTED
FALL TOMATOES
SERVES 6

5	TOMATOES (1¼ POUNDS/570 G)
3	CLOVES GARLIC, *finely minced*
¼	CUP (60 ML) OLIVE OIL
1	TABLESPOON MINCED FRESH THYME
1½	TEASPOONS SALT
½	TEASPOON FRESHLY GROUND BLACK PEPPER

Preheat the oven to 300°F (160°C).

Line a sheet pan with parchment paper. Quarter and seed the tomatoes and lay them on the parchment. In a bowl, mix the garlic and oil. Spoon the mixture over the tomatoes, dividing it equally among them and using all of it. Sprinkle the tomatoes with the thyme, salt, and pepper. Roast for 1 hour, or until caramelized and shriveled in appearance. Serve warm or at room temperature.

GARLIC CONFIT

MAKES ¾ CUP

12 CLOVES GARLIC, *peeled*

½ CUP (120 ML) OLIVE OIL

¼ TEASPOON SALT

1 STRIP LEMON PEEL, *about 2 inches (5 cm) long*

1 BAY LEAF

1 SPRIG OF THYME

Preheat the oven to 300°F (160°C).

Put the garlic in a small baking dish and cover with the oil. Make sure the garlic is fully submerged. Add the salt, lemon peel, bay leaf, and thyme. Cover with aluminum foil and roast for 35 minutes or until the garlic is lightly caramelized and soft. Serve warm or at room temperature. Any leftover garlic can be stored in the refrigerator for up to 5 days.

OVERLY RIPE, DARK BROWN, and aromatic, these are the bananas I reach for when making banana bread. In the northwest corner of the Greyfield garden, there is a thick, overgrown plot of banana trees. Tangled together, their abundant leaves are at their peak come late fall, but they only produce several "hands" of bananas, which taste best when left to deeply ripen. This sweet, tender banana bread is a great way to use an excess of bananas. The coffee butter is a rich, slightly bitter addition to balance this sweet treat.

Banana Walnut Bread

with Salted Coffee Butter

MAKES 2 LOAVES

5   BANANAS, OVERRIPE AND BROWN

3   CUPS (385 G) ALL-PURPOSE FLOUR

1   TEASPOON BAKING SODA

1½ TEASPOONS GROUND CINNAMON

1½ TEASPOONS GROUND ALLSPICE

1½ TEASPOONS GROUND GINGER

2   TEASPOONS SALT

½   CUP (1 STICK/115 G) BUTTER, *at room temperature, plus extra for the loaf pans*

½   CUP (120 ML) COCONUT OIL, *at room temperature*

1   CUP (220 G) PLUS 1 TABLESPOON DARK BROWN SUGAR

1   CUP (200 G) GRANULATED SUGAR

3   LARGE EGGS

1½ CUPS (180 G) TOASTED AND CHOPPED WALNUTS

1   CUP (240 ML) BUTTERMILK

2   TEASPOONS VANILLA EXTRACT

1   CUP (225 G) SALTED COFFEE BUTTER *(recipe follows)*

Preheat the oven to 350°F (175°C). Butter two 9 by 5-inch (23 by 12 cm) loaf pans and line the bottoms with parchment paper.

Peel 4 of the bananas and mash them together until smooth (you should have 2 cups/480 ml); set aside. In a small bowl, whisk together the flour, baking soda, cinnamon, allspice, ginger, and salt. Set aside.

In an electric mixer, use a paddle attachment to beat together the butter, coconut oil, 1 cup (220 g) brown sugar, and the granulated sugar until light and airy, about 3 minutes. Add the eggs and beat on low speed until combined.

Scrape the bottom and sides of the bowl. Add the flour mixture and mix until just combined. Add the mashed bananas, walnuts, buttermilk, and vanilla and mix until combined.

Equally divide the batter between the two loaf pans. Smooth with a spatula. Peel the remaining banana, cut in half lengthwise, and place each half on top of the batter in each pan. Sprinkle the remaining 1 tablespoon brown sugar over the banana slices. Bake until a skewer inserted in the center comes out clean, about 1 hour, rotating pans halfway through. Let the bread cool in the pans for 10 minutes, then remove from the pans and let cool completely on a wire rack. Serve with salted coffee butter.

Salted Coffee Butter MAKES 1 CUP (225 G)

1   CUP (2 STICKS/225 G) BUTTER, *at room temperature*

2   TABLESPOONS FRESHLY GROUND COFFEE BEANS

½   TEASPOON SALT

1   TEASPOON SORGHUM SYRUP *(you can substitute maple syrup or molasses)*

In a small pot over low heat, melt half of the butter. When the butter is hot, add the coffee and cook for 2 minutes. Remove from the heat and let steep for 3 minutes. Strain the melted butter through a fine-mesh sieve into a bowl, making sure to really press on the coffee grounds with the back of a spoon to extract all of the butter. Allow the coffee-infused butter to cool to room temperature. Mix in the remaining butter, the salt, and sorghum syrup. Stir well to combine. Serve at room temperature.

The butter can be made ahead and stored in the refrigerator for up to 1 week.

Smoked Fish and Potato Hash

SERVES 4

A BREAKFAST OF THIS MAGNITUDE requires love. Love meaning that you're willing to wake up early to make this, or do as I do and prep ahead. Smoked fish is a luxurious treat and a favored preservation method on the Atlantic coast. You can make your own following the instructions here, or you can sub in something available at your local grocery store: smoked trout or even a good-quality canned tuna. I recommend topping this with fried eggs or your preferred style—poached, scrambled, etc.

1	POUND (455 G) RED POTATOES
2	TABLESPOONS CANOLA OIL
2	TEASPOONS SALT
½	TEASPOON FRESHLY GROUND BLACK PEPPER
¼	CUP (55 G) BUTTER
2	SMALL ONIONS, *diced small (about 2 cups/250 g)*
1	RED BELL PEPPER, *diced small*
2	CLOVES GARLIC, *minced*
1	TEASPOON CHOPPED FRESH THYME
2	TEASPOONS CHOPPED FRESH PARSLEY
1	TEASPOON CHOPPED FRESH DILL
8	OUNCES (225 G) SMOKED SHEEPSHEAD *(recipe follows)*, *broken into pieces, or any kind of smoked fish*
1¼	CUPS (300 ML) HOLLANDAISE *(recipe follows)*

Preheat the oven to 350°F (175°C).

Cut the potatoes into a medium dice. In a large ovenproof sauté pan or large cast-iron pan, heat the oil over medium-high heat. Add the potatoes, 1 teaspoon of the salt, and the pepper. Sauté until the potatoes begin to get a little color, about 5 minutes. Place the pan in the oven and roast until tender, about 12 minutes.

While the potatoes are roasting, heat the butter in a large sauté pan over medium heat. When the butter is melted and slightly browned, add the onions. Cook the onions, stirring frequently, until they begin to lightly caramelize, about 10 minutes. Add the bell pepper, garlic, thyme, and the remaining 1 teaspoon salt. Continue to cook for about 4 minutes, stirring occasionally. Add the roasted potatoes, the parsley, and dill. Stir to combine. Gently stir in the smoked fish.

Scoop the hash into serving bowls. Top with a generous amount of hollandaise and a fried egg and serve immediately.

Hollandaise MAKES ABOUT 1¼ CUPS (300 ML)

1	CUP (2 STICKS/225 G) BUTTER
3	EGG YOLKS
2	TEASPOONS LEMON JUICE
1	TEASPOON TABASCO SAUCE
½	TEASPOON SALT

In a small pot, melt the butter over low heat. Set aside, keeping it warm.

In a small heatproof bowl, whisk together the egg yolks, lemon juice, Tabasco sauce, salt, and 1 tablespoon water. Place the bowl over a pot on the stove that has a small amount of simmering water. The water should not touch the bottom of the bowl. Whisk the egg mixture continually. Cook until the yolks are warm and have slightly thickened, about 3 minutes. Remove the bowl from the heat and set aside in a warm spot. Do not cook the eggs too long or they will turn into scrambled egg yolks and you will need to start over.

Remove the pot from the heat and dump out the water. Drape a towel over the opening and place the bowl on top (this will stabilize the bowl while you whisk). Whisking continuously, slowly drizzle the warm butter into the egg yolk mixture. Serve immediately.

Smoked Fish MAKES 8 TO 12 OUNCES
(225 TO 340 G)

- ½ CUP (120 ML) DRY WHITE WINE
- 1 CLOVE GARLIC, *smashed*

  ZEST OF ½ LEMON
- 1 TEASPOON WHOLE CORIANDER SEEDS
- 1 TEASPOON WHOLE BLACK PEPPERCORNS
- 2 BAY LEAVES
- 5 SPRIGS OF THYME
- 4 TABLESPOONS SALT
- 2 TABLESPOONS HONEY
- 8 TO 12 OUNCES (225 TO 340 G) FISH FILLETS
- 2 CUPS (140 G) WOOD CHIPS, *soaked in water*

In a medium pot, combine 1½ cups (360 ml) water, the wine, garlic, lemon zest, coriander, peppercorns, bay leaves, thyme, salt, and honey. Bring to a boil. Remove from the heat and let steep for 15 minutes. Add 1 cup (240 ml) ice water. Strain the brine into a container and cool in the refrigerator until cold. Discard the solids.

Submerge the fish into the chilled brine. Let the fish brine in the refrigerator for at least 2 hours and up to 6 hours.

Remove the fish from the brine and pat dry with paper towels.

Build a fire in a grill and let it burn down to low heat. Rake the coals in a pile on one side of the grill.

Put the fish on the grill grate, on the side with no coals directly underneath it. Add half of the soaked wood chips on top of the coals. When they begin to smoke, close the grill lid and cook slowly until the fish is cooked through to an internal temperature of 145°F (63°C), about 20 minutes. Replenish the wood chips as needed to maintain constant smoke. The fish can be served immediately, still hot from the grill, or cooled and stored in the refrigerator for up to 5 days.

BENNE SEED IS SESAME and sesame is benne for all practical purposes. But it is important to note that even this humble little seed can taste different based on quality. If you find "benne" seeds, odds are you are getting an heirloom variety. Anson Mills is my favorite producer of benne seeds. These plump little seeds have a pleasant nuttiness and a perfect little pop when eaten. I have been known to eat toasted benne by the spoonful. Ginger is a crop that grows beautifully on Cumberland and partners perfectly with benne to make a bright, complex dressing to pair with the bitter greens of fall.

Crisp Fall Green Salad

with Benne Seed Ginger Dressing

SERVES 6

1	BUNCH BABY KALE, *bottom of stems removed*
1	BUNCH DANDELION GREENS, *bottom of stems removed*
1	HEAD OF LETTUCE, *leaves separated*
8	BABY CARROTS, *peeled if needed, thinly shaved on a mandoline*
1	KOHLRABI, *peeled, thinly shaved on a mandoline*
5	BRUSSELS SPROUTS, *thinly shaved on a mandoline*
	PINCH OF FLAKY SEA SALT
1	CUP (240 ML) BENNE SEED GINGER DRESSING *(recipe follows)*

Benne Seed Ginger Dressing MAKES 1 CUP (240 ML)

1½	TABLESPOONS MINCED GINGER
¼	CUP (15 G) CHOPPED SCALLION
½	CLOVE GARLIC, *chopped*
3	TABLESPOONS BENNE SEEDS, *toasted*
¼	CUP (60 ML) UNSEASONED RICE VINEGAR
1	TABLESPOON SOY SAUCE
½	TEASPOON HONEY
¾	CUP (180 ML) GRAPESEED OIL

Wash and dry the kale, dandelion greens, and lettuce. Transfer the greens to a serving bowl. Top the greens with the carrots, kohlrabi, and Brussels sprouts. Sprinkle the salt over the salad. Toss the salad with the benne seed dressing in the bowl, or serve it on the side.

Put the ginger, scallion, garlic, benne seeds, vinegar, soy sauce, and honey in a blender. Puree until smooth. With the blender running on low speed, slowly add the grapeseed oil. The dressing can be stored in the refrigerator for up to 5 days.

Notes on a
CHEESE BOARD

Give me a luscious triple cream sitting in a pool of honey, spooned over a crusty slice of bread. Or a dense and salty blue, with its crumbling ridges, served with a sweet and earthy fig jam. Nutty and subtle tomme, with briny, crunchy summer pickles. There is no wrong way to eat or serve cheese. A simple lunch for two or a course for dinner, cheese is an easy way to share something spectacular without spending inordinate amounts of time in the kitchen.

INTERESTING SOUTHERN CHEESE PRODUCERS

During the past ten years, the number of cheesemakers in the South has grown extensively. Here are a few of the cheeses and creameries that are leading the way for southern artisan cheesemakers, but this list is not exhaustive. Be on the lookout at your local farmers' market for small producers that are making cheese from pasture-raised animals. All of the creameries listed make multiple cheeses that are worthy of your attention.

CREAMERY: BLACKBERRY FARM, TENNESSEE
Cheese to try: Brebis (seasonal)

I particularly love the Brebis, a sheep's milk cheese that is similar in texture to ricotta. Sheep's milk naturally has the highest fat content of any of the milks used for making cheese, which gives the cheeses a rich and supple texture.

CREAMERY: BOXCARR CREAMERY, NORTH CAROLINA
Cheese to try: Rocket's Robiola

With a bloomy, ashed rind, this cheese has the rich, creamy texture of a triple cream with an earthy maturity that reveal hints of mushroom. As it ages the cheese gets softer and slightly more buttery.

CREAMERY: SEQUATCHIE COVE CREAMERY, TENNESSEE
Cheese to try: Shakerag Blue

Wrapped in fig leaves that have been dipped in Tennessee whiskey, this blue has a complex flavor and pleasantly salty punch.

CREAMERY: SWEET GRASS DAIRY, GEORGIA
Cheese to try: Green Hill

Sweet Grass was one of the first southern cheese producers I grew to know and love. Green Hill has been on my cheese boards ever since. Soft and buttery, half a wheel and a pile of garden greens make for an indulgent snack.

CREAMERY: MEADOW CREEK DAIRY, VIRGINIA
Cheese to try: Appalachian

Complex and earthy, with slightly nutty notes, this cheese reminds me of a raclette. Another added bonus: It is my all-time favorite for making a grilled cheese.

WHEN WHOLE-ROASTED IN COALS, sweet potatoes pick up a caramelized, smoky note while developing a custardy consistency. Whipped with cream and butter, they turn into velvet. I like adding a bit of heat with some Espelette pepper, but you could go a sweeter route and garnish it with a dusting of cinnamon, or the coffee butter on page 241, instead.

Coal-Roasted Sweet Potatoes

SERVES 4 TO 6

3   POUNDS (1.4 KG) SWEET POTATOES *(see Notes)*

½   CUP (120 ML) HEAVY CREAM

1   SPRIG OF THYME

2   BAY LEAVES

½   CUP (1 STICK/115 G) BUTTER

1   TEASPOON SALT

½   TEASPOON ESPELETTE PEPPER

NOTES *When making this recipe, make sure to adjust cooking times for size. This recipe was made using small sweet potatoes that were grown on Cumberland. Your standard grocery store sweet potato will be a little larger and need a little extra time to cook.*

If you can't cook the sweet potatoes on a grill, you can use your oven. Preheat the oven to 375°F (190°C). Place the sweet potatoes on a baking sheet and cook until very tender and soft on the inside, about 30 minutes. Let cool slightly before peeling the skins off and adding the pulp to the food processor.

Build a fire in a grill and let it burn down to low heat (see Notes).

Nestle the sweet potatoes into the coals and close the lid. Cook until soft and easily pierced with a wooden skewer, about 30 minutes, flipping them over halfway through cooking. Remove the sweet potatoes from the coals and set aside.

In a small pot over low heat, combine the cream, thyme, and bay leaves. Bring to a simmer. Remove from the heat and set aside, allowing the herbs to steep in the cream for 10 to 15 minutes. Strain the cream through a fine-mesh sieve. Place the herb-infused cream and the butter in a small pot over low heat to combine until the butter is melted. Remove from the heat.

Dust any remaining ash off the sweet potatoes using a kitchen towel and peel the skins off. Put the sweet potato pulp in a food processor. Add the warm cream mixture and the salt. Pulse until smooth. Garnish with Espelette pepper and serve.

Sea Island Red Pea Chili

SEA ISLAND RED PEAS, Geechee red peas, and Sapelo peas are regional names for a particular type of cowpea that originated in West Africa. These creamy and hearty little peas are hand harvested and dried, turning a brick red and imparting the same ruddy color to the broth they're cooked in. They are more famously known as the original cowpea used in hoppin' john, a dish of rice and peas with African origins. I like to use them to make a hearty fall chili.

SERVES 6

3 TABLESPOONS CANOLA OIL

2 POUNDS (910 G) GROUND BEEF

1 ONION, *diced small*

4 CLOVES GARLIC, *minced*

2 JALAPEÑOS, *seeded and minced*

¾ TEASPOON GROUND CUMIN

½ TEASPOON SWEET PAPRIKA

1 TEASPOON DRIED OREGANO

2 TEASPOONS CHILE POWDER (*I like Chimayo or ancho*)

2 TABLESPOONS TOMATO PASTE

2 CHIPOTLES IN ADOBO, *minced*

1 TABLESPOON ADOBO SAUCE (*from the can*)

1 CUP (240 ML) BEER, *lager style*

1 (28-OUNCE/795 G) CAN DICED TOMATOES

4 CUPS (715 G) COOKED SEA ISLAND RED PEAS (*recipe follows*)

1 CUP (240 ML) PEA COOKING LIQUID, *reserved from cooking*

3 CUPS (720 ML) CHICKEN STOCK

4 TEASPOONS SALT

SLICED SCALLIONS, SHREDDED SHARP CHEDDAR CHEESE, AND SOUR CREAM (*optional*)

In a large pot, heat 2 tablespoons of the oil over medium heat. Add the beef and cook until lightly browned, about 6 minutes. Remove the beef from the pot and set aside. Pour off the fat.

In the same pot, heat the remaining 1 tablespoon oil over medium-low heat. Add the onion, garlic, and jalapeño. Cook gently for 5 minutes, until the onion is translucent. Turn up the heat to medium. Add the cumin, paprika, oregano, chile powder, tomato paste, chipotles, and adobo sauce. Cook for 1 minute, stirring to coat the vegetables in the tomato paste. Add the beer and stir. Simmer for 2 minutes. Add the tomatoes, beef, peas, pea cooking liquid, and stock. Bring to a simmer, then reduce the heat to low. Cook for 1 hour, uncovered, stirring occasionally. Season with the salt. Serve topped with scallions, cheddar, sour cream, or any of your favorite toppings.

Sea Island Red Peas MAKES 4 CUPS (715 G)

1½ CUPS (290 G) DRIED SEA ISLAND RED PEAS (*if using an alternative bean, adjust cooking time and quantity of water, as needed*)

1 BAY LEAF

1 CLOVE GARLIC

¼ ONION, *cut into a wedge*

2 TEASPOONS SALT

In a medium pot, cover the peas, bay leaf, garlic, onion, and salt with 6 cups (1.4 L) water. Bring to a boil, then reduce the heat to a gentle simmer. Cover and cook for 45 minutes, stirring occasionally, until tender. Let the peas cool in their cooking liquid until ready to use. Pick out the garlic and onion and discard. Reserve 1 cup (240 ml) of the cooking liquid.

Grilled Cauliflower

with Crunchy
Garlic Chile Oil

SERVES 4

I EAT A LOT of vegetables. This dish is a good excuse to bypass meat as the main course and opt for a vegetarian dinner. Cauliflower is a particularly good focal point for an all-veggie dinner, since it is crunchy and slightly sweet and pairs well with a range of flavors. Roasted over a wood fire, it picks up a gentle smoky note that is extremely satisfying. Warning: You will love the crunchy garlic chile oil and you will always want to have it around your house as a condiment. I highly recommend making a double batch.

1	HEAD OF CAULIFLOWER
2	TABLESPOONS OLIVE OIL
1	TEASPOON SALT
½	TEASPOON FRESHLY GROUND BLACK PEPPER
1	TABLESPOON CHOPPED FRESH PARSLEY
¼	CUP (60 ML) CRUNCHY GARLIC CHILE OIL *(recipe follows)*

Build a fire in a grill and let it burn down to medium heat (see Note).

Cut the whole head of cauliflower into slices ½ inch (12 mm) thick. Coat with the olive oil, salt, and pepper. Place the cauliflower slices on the grill grate in a single layer. Cover and cook for 10 to 15 minutes, flipping halfway through the cooking process. You want each side to have a nice char and the cauliflower to be tender. Remove from the grill and toss with the parsley and chile oil. The cauliflower will naturally break into small pieces as it is tossed. Serve hot. I recommend serving a little extra chile oil on the side.

NOTE *If you can't cook the cauliflower on a grill, you can use your oven. Preheat the oven to 400°F (205°C). Heat a large cast-iron pan over medium-high heat. Cut the whole head of cauliflower into slices ½ inch (12 mm) thick. Coat with the olive oil, salt, and pepper. Place the cauliflower slices into the cast-iron pan in a single layer and sear until lightly charred, about 4 minutes. Flip the cauliflower over and transfer the pan to the oven. Cook until cauliflower is tender and caramelized, about 8 minutes. Remove from the pan and toss with the parsley and chile oil.*

Crunchy Garlic Chile Oil MAKES ½ CUP (120 ML)

¼	CUP (60 ML) OLIVE OIL
¼	CUP (60 ML) CANOLA OIL
7	CLOVES GARLIC, *minced*
¼	TEASPOON SALT
1	TABLESPOON ALEPPO CHILE
¼	TEASPOON SWEET PAPRIKA

In a small pot over medium-low heat, combine the olive oil, canola oil, garlic, and salt. Bring to a gentle simmer and cook until the garlic is a light golden brown, about 10 minutes. Remove from the heat and stir in the Aleppo chile and paprika. Let cool to room temperature. It can be made ahead and stored at room temperature for up to 1 month.

LAYERED WITH SPICES, PEPPERS, and herbs, this dish is inspired by the multitude of Caribbean and South American cooks who have helped to transform Florida's culinary identity. The sweet and flaky grouper is simmered in the aromatic broth with hints of ginger and garlic. Ladled over coconut rice, it becomes the perfect comfort food and an easy meal to share with friends.

Caribbean-Style Fish Stew

with Coconut Rice, Peanuts, and Cilantro

SERVES 4

- 1 POUND (455 G) GROUPER FILLET, *skin removed and cut into 8 pieces*
- 2½ TEASPOONS SALT
- 2 TABLESPOONS COCONUT OIL
- ½ WHITE ONION, *diced small*
- 3 CLOVES GARLIC, *minced*
- 2 CUBANELLE PEPPERS, *seeded and diced small*
- 1 HABANERO PEPPER, *seeded and diced small*
- 2 TABLESPOONS PEELED AND MINCED FRESH GINGER
- 1 TEASPOON GROUND TURMERIC
- ½ TEASPOON GROUND ALLSPICE
- ½ TEASPOON GROUND CORIANDER
- ½ TEASPOON SWEET PAPRIKA
- ¼ TEASPOON GROUND CUMIN
- ¼ TEASPOON FRESHLY GROUND BLACK PEPPER
- 1 BAY LEAF
- 12 OUNCES (360 ML) BEER, *preferably lager style*
- 1½ CUPS (360 ML) CANNED TOMATOES, *pureed*
- 1 CUP (240 ML) CLAM JUICE
- 1 TABLESPOON CHOPPED FRESH CILANTRO

  JUICE OF ½ LIME
- 5 CUPS (775 G) COCONUT RICE *(recipe follows)*
- ½ CUP (70 G) CRUSHED ROASTED, SALTED PEANUTS

Season the grouper with 1 teaspoon of the salt. In a large sauté pan, heat the coconut oil over medium-high heat. Add the grouper to the pan and sear until golden brown on one side, about 3 minutes. Flip the fish over and cook for an additional minute. Remove the fish from the pan and set aside.

Reduce the heat to medium and add the onion, garlic, Cubanelle peppers, habanero pepper, and ginger to the pan and sauté until soft, about 3 minutes. Add the turmeric, allspice, coriander, paprika, cumin, black pepper, and bay leaf and cook for 1 minute while stirring. Add the beer and bring to a simmer; cook for 3 minutes. Add the tomato puree, clam juice, and the remaining 1½ teaspoons salt and bring to a simmer. Cook for 5 minutes.

Return the grouper to the pan and cook until just done, 8 to 10 minutes (depending on the thickness of the fish). Stir in the cilantro and lime juice.

To serve, ladle the stew over the rice. Garnish with the peanuts.

Coconut Rice MAKES 5 CUPS (775 G)

- 1½ CUPS (275 G) CAROLINA GOLD RICE
- 1¾ CUPS (420 ML) COCONUT MILK
- 1 TABLESPOON COCONUT OIL
- 1 TEASPOON SALT

Put the rice in a bowl, cover with cold water, and stir with your hand—the water will turn cloudy from the starch in the rice. Drain the rice in a fine-mesh sieve and return the rice to the bowl. Repeat this process until the water becomes fairly clear, about five passes. Let the rice drain in the sieve and set aside.

In a small pot, bring the coconut milk, ½ cup (120 ml) water, the coconut oil, and salt to a boil over high heat. Stir in the rice, bring back to a boil, and cover. Reduce the heat to low and cook for 15 minutes. Remove from the heat and let rest, covered, for 5 minutes. Fluff the rice with a fork and serve.

Spaghetti Squash

with Pecorino Romano Cream and Walnuts

I'VE ALWAYS BEEN AMAZED by the ubiquity of spaghetti squash. Of all the amazing varieties of squash, how did it become a grocery store staple? For years I paid no attention to this humble little squash. One day Ben suggested we put it on the menu. I brushed it off. Spaghetti squash? Bah, humbug! But Ben persisted, and as he often can be, he was right. Roasted and pulled into its namesake strands, it came alive when tossed in a rich, creamy Pecorino Romano–laden sauce and topped with crushed walnuts and fresh parsley. From ho-hum to *magnifique*. For extra depth, try adding a little crunchy garlic chile oil (page 252).

SERVES 2 AS A MAIN COURSE OR 4 AS A SIDE

- 1 SPAGHETTI SQUASH (ABOUT 2 POUNDS/910 G)
- 1 TABLESPOON OLIVE OIL
- ½ TEASPOON CHILE FLAKES
- 1 TEASPOON BUTTER
- 4 CUPS (260 G) STEMMED AND CHOPPED CURLY KALE
- 2 TEASPOONS LEMON JUICE
- 1 TEASPOON SALT
- 1 CUP (240 ML) PECORINO ROMANO CREAM *(recipe follows)*
- ¼ CUP (25 G) WALNUTS, *roasted, salted, and lightly crushed*
- 1 TEASPOON CHOPPED FRESH PARSLEY

Pecorino Romano Cream MAKES 1 CUP (240 ML)

- 1 TABLESPOON BUTTER
- 2 TEASPOONS MINCED SHALLOT
- 2 TEASPOONS MINCED GARLIC
- 1¾ CUPS (420 ML) HEAVY CREAM
- ½ CUP FINELY GRATED PECORINO ROMANO CHEESE
-   PINCH OF FRESHLY GROUND BLACK PEPPER
- ¼ TEASPOON SALT
- ¼ TEASPOON SHERRY VINEGAR

Preheat the oven to 350°F (175°C).

Cut the spaghetti squash in half lengthwise and scoop out all of the seeds. Place the squash, cut side down, on a sheet pan. Roast for 20 minutes. The interior should be firm, but easily pulled into strands with a fork. Using a fork, gently scrape the squash from side to side into long strands. Set aside.

In a medium sauté pan, heat the oil over medium heat. Add the chile flakes and sauté for 10 seconds. Add the butter, kale, lemon juice, and ½ teaspoon of the salt. Cook until tender, stirring frequently. Add the spaghetti squash strands and the remaining ½ teaspoon salt. Stir to incorporate. Transfer to a serving bowl and mix with the Pecorino Romano cream. Garnish with the walnuts and parsley and serve.

In a medium saucepan, melt the butter over low heat. Add the shallot and garlic and cook gently until soft, being careful not to let them brown, about 3 minutes. Add the cream. Bring to a simmer and reduce for 10 minutes. Add the cheese, pepper, salt, and vinegar. Whisk to incorporate the cheese. Remove from the heat and keep warm until ready to use. Any leftover sauce can be stored in the refrigerator for up to 5 days.

A Lesson in Hospitality and
BONE COLLECTING

My favorite table on Cumberland Island sits modestly under a pergola of jasmine. A dinner invitation is needed to reach it. Upon arrival at the home in which it sits, you are greeted by a reconstructed horse skeleton hanging at the front door. Entering this house of curios, your focus will inevitably land on a whale vertebra mobile, suspended from the ceiling in the center of the room, then over to a fossilized megalodon tooth nestled among pottery shards and various animal bones. Through a screen door and out to a patio that hugs the home, you are greeted by sweeping views of the salt marsh and a tennis court that looks half consumed by the maritime forest. A palm tree grows right in the middle of the deck. My favorite table sits here, where I learned some of the greatest rules of hospitality, as taught by Gogo Ferguson and Dave Sayre.

The arts of bone collecting and jewelry making are Gogo's most famed talents, but it is her hospitality that I grew to admire and study. Most notable social events on the island are hosted at Gogo and Dave's home. At their table, there is always room for another seat to be pulled up. The oysters that go on the grill must always be from Cumberland, tequila or mezcal is the drink of choice, and the living room is often a stage for traveling musicians. There is usually a guest from some far-off destination sharing stories of adventure and travel. Dave and Gogo would happily light a fire under the grill and invite Ben and I over, after a long day in the kitchen, for endless piles of oysters, drinks, and stories. This is the table I hope to continue to create, wherever I may be—a table where all are welcomed, as long as you are willing to share a story and a drink.

Caramelized Pumpkin

with Guajillo Chile and Spiced Yogurt

SERVES 4

IN OCTOBER 2016, I found myself in northeast Georgia having evacuated Cumberland Island fleeing Hurricane Matthew. Between staring intently at hurricane updates and pacing around the house, I caught wind of a local farmer with an excess of Musquee de Provence pumpkins, a hard-to-find heirloom variety. The impracticality of returning to Cumberland with 150 pounds of heirloom pumpkin never crossed my mind. I hardly had enough room in my car! Later that month I served the pumpkin at a James Beard dinner in Atlanta, Sunday Supper South, with mole negro. That dish inspired the iteration below. The guajillo chile sauce is a beautiful companion to the slightly sweet, caramelized pumpkin. Seminole pumpkins are a little easier to find in this hot, humid climate, but any pumpkin or winter squash would work well in this recipe.

1	(4-POUND/1.8 KG) SEMINOLE PUMPKIN, or other winter squash variety
1	TABLESPOON OLIVE OIL
1¼	TEASPOONS SALT
5	SPRIGS OF THYME
¼	CUP (40 G) BENNE SEED
¼	TEASPOON PLUS 2 TABLESPOONS CANOLA OIL
1	TABLESPOON BUTTER
1	CUP (240 ML) GUAJILLO CHILE SAUCE (recipe follows)
¼	CUP (60 ML) SPICED YOGURT (recipe follows)
1	TABLESPOON CHOPPED FRESH CILANTRO
1	TABLESPOON FINELY GRATED MANCHEGO CHEESE

Preheat the oven to 350°F (175°C).

Cut the pumpkin in half and remove the seeds. Cut into 8 thick slices. Toss in the olive oil and season with 1 teaspoon of the salt. Spread on a sheet pan in a single layer and top with the thyme sprigs. Roast until tender and easily pierced with the tip of a knife, about 30 minutes.

While the pumpkin is roasting, in a bowl, mix the benne seed, the remaining ¼ teaspoon salt, and ¼ teaspoon of the canola oil. In a small pan over medium-low heat, cook the seasoned benne seed, stirring frequently, until lightly toasted and fragrant, about 3 minutes. Set aside.

In a large sauté pan, heat the remaining 2 tablespoons canola oil and the butter over medium heat. Add the cooked pumpkin and sear until caramelized, 3 to 4 minutes on each side. Remove from the pan.

Garnish the caramelized pumpkin with the chile sauce, spiced yogurt, cilantro, cheese, and toasted benne seed and serve hot.

Guajillo Chile Sauce MAKES 2 CUPS (480 ML)

5	DRIED GUAJILLO CHILES, stemmed and seeded
2	DRIED ANCHO CHILES, stemmed and seeded
3	CUPS (720 ML) HOT WATER
1	TEASPOON CANOLA OIL
¼	ONION, sliced
2	CLOVES GARLIC, sliced
1	TABLESPOON BENNE SEED
¼	TOMATO, chopped
¼	TEASPOON FRESHLY GROUND BLACK PEPPER
¼	TEASPOON GROUND CINNAMON
¼	TEASPOON GROUND ALLSPICE
1	CUP (240 ML) BREWED COFFEE
1½	TEASPOONS SALT
1	TABLESPOON HONEY

In a dry pan over medium-high heat, toast the guajillo chiles and ancho chiles, flipping often, until lightly charred and fragrant, about 2 minutes. Put the chiles in a bowl and cover with the hot water. Place a small plate on top of the chiles to keep them submerged and let soak for 20 minutes. Remove chiles from water and set aside. Reserve 1½ cups (360 ml) of the chile-soaking water.

In a medium pot, heat the oil over medium heat. Add the onion, garlic, and benne seed. Cook for about 3 minutes, stirring frequently.

Add the tomato, black pepper, cinnamon, and allspice. Cook until the liquid from the tomato has nearly evaporated, about 5 minutes. Transfer mixture to a blender with the coffee, soaked chiles, and reserved chile water. Puree until completely smooth. Return the mixture to the pot and bring to a boil. Reduce to a simmer and cook for 15 minutes, stirring occasionally, until the sauce has thickened slightly. Add the salt and honey. This sauce can be made ahead and stored in the refrigerator for up to 5 days. It can also be frozen for up to 1 month.

Spiced Yogurt MAKES ¾ CUP (180 ML)

½	CUP (120 ML) PLAIN YOGURT
2	TABLESPOONS LIME JUICE
¼	TEASPOON GROUND CORIANDER
¼	TEASPOON GROUND CUMIN
½	TEASPOON HONEY
¼	TEASPOON SALT

In a bowl, combine all of the ingredients and 1 tablespoon water. Store in the refrigerator for up to 1 week.

BRAISING IS ONE OF my favorite cooking techniques. I love that you can prep the ingredients, place them in the oven, and walk away. The long, slow cooking process tenderizes pork, making it meltingly tender and indulgent. This recipe is a nod to the influence of the beautiful Cuban-style braised pork dishes I have enjoyed. When in Miami, I love to swing by Versailles (a legendary Cuban restaurant in Little Havana) and get the Cuban braised pork shoulder. They serve it topped with extra-crispy *chicharrons*, which would be a decadent addition to this recipe as well.

Slow-Braised Pork Shoulder

with
Citrus, Peppers,
and Beer

SERVES 4

3	POUNDS (1.4 KG) BONELESS PORK SHOULDER, *cut into 8 equal pieces*
1½	TABLESPOONS SALT
1	TEASPOON FRESHLY GROUND BLACK PEPPER
2	TEASPOONS DRIED OREGANO
½	TEASPOON SWEET PAPRIKA
½	TEASPOON GROUND CINNAMON
½	TEASPOON GROUND GINGER
1	TABLESPOON CANOLA OIL
2	CUBANELLE OR POBLANO PEPPERS, *sliced*
1	WHITE ONION, *thinly sliced*
7	CLOVES GARLIC, *chopped*
1	SMALL TOMATO, *chopped*
1	CUP (240 ML) BEER, *lager or ale style*
1	CUP (240 ML) CHICKEN STOCK
½	ORANGE, *sliced into half-moons*
1	LIME, *sliced into half-moons*
	SMALL HANDFUL OF FRESH CILANTRO LEAVES AND STEMS, *plus chopped fresh cilantro for serving (optional)*
2	BAY LEAVES

Preheat the oven to 300°F (150°C).

Season the pork with the salt, black pepper, oregano, paprika, cinnamon, and ginger. Let marinate for 15 minutes. In a large Dutch oven, or ovenproof pot, heat the oil over medium-high heat. Add the pork and sear to golden brown, about 6 minutes on each side. Once the pork is evenly seared and caramelized, remove from the pot and set aside.

Add the Cubanelle peppers, onion, garlic, and tomato to the pot and cook, stirring regularly, until lightly caramelized, about 5 minutes. Remove the vegetables from the pot and set aside. Add the beer to the pot and bring to a boil; cook for 2 minutes. Add the stock and bring to a simmer. Return the pork to the pot in a single layer, and top with the sautéed pepper and onion mixture. Add the orange, lime, cilantro, and bay leaves. Cover the pot with the lid and transfer to the oven. Cook until the pork is fork tender, about 1 hour and 45 minutes.

Let the pork cool in the braising liquid for 30 minutes. Remove the pork from the pot and set aside. Strain the braising liquid through a fine-mesh sieve into a bowl; you should have about 2 cups (480 ml) liquid. Discard the solids. Skim the excess fat from the liquid. Put the liquid in a small pot and bring to a simmer over medium heat. Reduce by half.

While the liquid is reducing, pick through the pork and remove any excess fat from the meat. Put pork shoulder in a small roasting pan and cover with the reduced braising liquid. Heat in the oven for 5 to 8 minutes, until the pork is warmed through. Transfer the pork to a serving platter, spoon the reduced braising liquid over it, sprinkle with chopped cilantro, and serve.

Banana Leaf–Wrapped Snapper

with Radish Salsa

SERVES 4 TO 6

THERE IS SOMETHING QUITE GRATIFYING and efficient about cooking in a banana leaf. Wrapping a beautiful fresh fish fillet into a perfect little package, cooking over fire, and then presenting this gift to your guests is its own moment of magic. The banana leaf imparts a slightly sweet aroma to the flesh of the fish and releases its perfume when you open the leaf to reveal the flaky buttered snapper that has been perfectly steamed within. Banana leaves grow abundantly in the tropical South. The rustic nature of this type of cooking is soulful, and utilizing the natural elements in my surroundings is one of my favorite ways to cook. If you don't have a banana tree, banana leaves can also easily be found in Latin American or Asian markets.

2	LARGE BANANA LEAVES, *about 15 inches (38 cm) long and 8 inches (20 cm) wide*
2	(1-POUND/455 G) SNAPPER FILLETS
1½	TEASPOONS SALT
½	CUP (120 ML) KEY LIME CORIANDER BUTTER, *at room temperature (recipe follows)*
1	CUP (240 ML) RADISH SALSA *(recipe follows)*
	KEY LIMES

Build a fire in a grill and let it burn down to low heat (see Note).

Prepare the banana leaf by trimming away any hard stem. Cut two thin strips that you can use to tie the banana leaf package closed. Pass the leaf over an open flame on low. This will make the banana leaf more pliable.

Season the snapper fillets with the salt. Lay one of the banana leaves flat, and place one of the snapper fillets in the middle of the leaf. Spread half of the lime coriander butter on the fish. Wrap the fish by folding over lengthwise and then folding over the two sides. Use one of the thin strips to tie the wrapping closed (see image on page 31). You want to make sure that the package is secured so that as the fish cooks, the steam stays in the banana leaf and the melted butter pools at the bottom. Repeat with the second snapper fillet.

Place the banana leaf–wrapped fish on the grill grate. The coals should be white hot with no flame. Cover the grill and cook for 20 minutes, until the fish is cooked through to an internal temperature of 145°F (63°C).

Serve the fish in the banana leaf with a side of the radish salsa and a few Key limes.

NOTE *If you can't cook the snapper on a grill, you can use your oven. Preheat the oven to 325°F (165°C). Place the banana leaf–wrapped fish on a baking sheet and cook until the fish is cooked through with an internal temperature of 145°F (63°C), about 18 minutes.*

Key Lime Coriander Butter

MAKES ½ CUP (120 ML)

½	CUP (1 STICK/115 G) BUTTER, *at room temperature*
½	SHALLOT, *finely minced*
1	CLOVE GARLIC, *finely minced*
1	TEASPOON KEY LIME ZEST
2	TEASPOONS KEY LIME JUICE
1	TABLESPOON MINCED FRESH CILANTRO
½	TEASPOON GROUND CORIANDER
½	TEASPOON SALT

In a bowl, mix all of the ingredients together until well incorporated. The butter can be made ahead and stored in the refrigerator for up to 5 days.

Radish Salsa MAKES 1 CUP (240 ML)

3	RED RADISHES (ABOUT 6 OUNCES/170 G), *diced small*
2	TABLESPOONS MINCED FRESH CILANTRO
1	TABLESPOON OLIVE OIL
2	TEASPOONS FRESH LIME JUICE
½	TEASPOON SALT

In a bowl, mix all of the ingredients together until well combined. Salsa can be made ahead and stored in the refrigerator for up to 3 days.

SHRIMP AND GRITS ARE ICONIC in Low Country cooking. It's hard to think of another dish that has the same grasp on the culinary identity of this region. Fish and grits, though, that's a different story, and while equally alluring, it has remained in the shadows of its more famous counterpart. During my first winter on the barrier islands, on a particularly cold and blustery day, I was treated to a simple meal of cornmeal-dredged flounder served over buttery grits. Hearty and warming, this dish has been a favorite of mine since. This is my heartfelt rendition of classic Low County cooking. The shrimp is turned into a butter, which gets stirred into rice grits, a broken rice grain. The flounder is seared to a perfect golden brown and garnished with lemon and flaky sea salt, and ideally should be served with an ice-cold beer.

Fish, Shrimp, and Grits, Oh My!

SERVES 4

½ CUP (120 ML) MILK

1½ TEASPOONS KOSHER SALT, *plus more for the flounder*

1 BAY LEAF

½ CUP (90 G) RICE GRITS

1¼ CUPS (235 G) SHRIMP BUTTER *(recipe follows)*

2 TABLESPOONS CANOLA OIL

4 (5-OUNCE/140 G) FLOUNDER FILLETS

2 TEASPOONS LEMON JUICE

1 TEASPOON CHOPPED FRESH PARSLEY

1 LEMON, *cut into wedges*

PINCH OF SEA SALT

Shrimp Butter MAKES 1¼ CUPS (235 G)

½ CUP (1 STICK/115 G) BUTTER

1 CLOVE GARLIC, *minced*

8 OUNCES (225 G) SHRIMP, *peeled and cleaned*

¼ TEASPOON CAYENNE POWDER

¼ TEASPOON PAPRIKA

¼ TEASPOON FRESHLY GROUND BLACK PEPPER

1 TEASPOON SALT

¼ CUP (60 ML) DRY WHITE WINE

¼ TEASPOON TABASCO SAUCE

¼ TEASPOON WORCESTERSHIRE SAUCE

In a medium pot, combine 2½ cups (600 ml) water, the milk, kosher salt, and bay leaf. Bring to a boil over medium heat. Stir in the rice grits. Reduce the heat to a simmer and cook for about 16 minutes, stirring frequently. When the rice grits are cooked though, add 1 cup (190 g) of the shrimp butter. Stir to combine. Remove from heat and keep warm until ready to serve.

While the rice grits are cooking, lightly season the flounder with a pinch of kosher salt for each fillet. Heat the oil in a large sauté pan or cast-iron pan over medium-high heat. When the oil is hot, add the fillets in a single layer. Make sure there is room between the fish fillets. Cook for 2 to 3 minuets, letting the fish sear to a nice golden brown. Flip and sear until cooked through, about 1 minute. Remove the fish from the pan. Pour off the excess oil. To the pan, add the remaining ¼ cup (45 g) shrimp butter, the lemon juice, and parsley to make a quick pan sauce.

To serve, spoon the rice grits into serving bowls. Top with the flounder fillets and pan sauce. Serve with the lemon wedges and sea salt.

In a large sauté pan over medium heat, melt half of the butter. Add the garlic and cook for 1 minute. Add the shrimp, cayenne, paprika, black pepper, and salt. Cook until just barely done, about 2 minutes. Use a slotted spoon to transfer the shrimp to a food processor. Return the pan to the heat and deglaze with the wine. Reduce by half. Add the reduced wine, Tabasco sauce, Worcestershire sauce, and the remaining butter to the food processor. Pulse until smooth. Set aside until ready to use. Shrimp butter can be made ahead and stored in the refrigerator for up to 5 days.

Fried Apple Pie

with Salted Rum Caramel

MAKES 10 PIES

APPLES ARE SYNONYMOUS WITH FALL and I am always happy to bring them into the kitchen during this season, especially when I can get varieties like Arkansas Black, with its crisp texture and tart, sweet flavor. Ben is often making variations of fried pies, perfecting his crust along the way. Thankfully, we get to relish in his hard work! The crispy, flaky crust is topped with a sprinkle of cinnamon and sugar. Making the filling one day ahead is a nice way to streamline the cooking process.

4   APPLES

½   TEASPOON GROUND CINNAMON

¼   TEASPOON GROUND GINGER

¼   TEASPOON GROUND ALLSPICE

3   TABLESPOONS BROWN SUGAR

3   TABLESPOONS GRANULATED SUGAR

½   TEASPOON VANILLA EXTRACT

¼   CUP (60 ML) DARK RUM

    PINCH OF SALT

1   TABLESPOON BUTTER

10 (5-INCH/12 CM) ROUNDS CHILLED PIE DOUGH *(recipe follows), plus flour for dusting*

1   EGG, *lightly beaten with 1 tablespoon water*

6   CUPS (1.4 L) CANOLA OIL

3   TABLESPOONS CINNAMON-SUGAR, *for dusting (recipe follows)*

½   CUP (120 ML) SALTED RUM CARAMEL *(recipe follows)*

    VANILLA ICE CREAM

Peel and core the apples, and small dice them. Set ½ cup (80 g) aside. In a medium pot, combine the remaining apples, the cinnamon, ginger, allspice, brown sugar, granulated sugar, vanilla, rum, salt, and ¼ cup (60 ml) water. Cook over medium-low heat, stirring often, until thickened and jam-like, about 18 minutes. Add the reserved apples and cook for 5 minutes. Stir in the butter and remove the apple filling from the heat (you should have about 2 cups of filling). Refrigerate until cold.

To assemble the pies, lightly flour your work surface and place the pie rounds on top. Place about 2½ tablespoons filling in the center of each dough round. Use your fingers to spread a small amount of egg wash around the edges of the pie dough. Fold the dough over the filling and press to seal with your fingers. When you have completed all the pies, use the tip of a fork to crimp the sealed edges. (This will ensure the dough is sealed). Cut two slits into the top of each pie. Place the pies on a kitchen towel–lined baking sheet and keep chilled until ready to fry.

In a medium pot, heat the oil to 350°F (175°C).

When the oil is ready, add the pies, 3 at a time, and fry until deep golden brown, about 5 minutes. Transfer to a paper towel–lined baking sheet and immediately sprinkle each pie with a healthy pinch of the cinnamon-sugar. Serve warm with a drizzle of the caramel and the ice cream.

Alternatively, you can bake the pies. Preheat the oven to 350°F (175°C). Place the pies on a parchment–lined baking sheet. Brush each pie with the egg wash and sprinkle with cinnamon-sugar. Bake until golden brown and the filling is bubbling, about 25 minutes.

Pie Dough MAKES 10 (5-INCH/12 CM) ROUNDS

3   CUPS (385 G) ALL-PURPOSE FLOUR, *plus more for dusting*

1½ TEASPOONS SALT

1½ TEASPOONS SUGAR

¾   CUP (1½ STICKS/170 G) COLD BUTTER, *diced*

½   CUP (120 ML) PLUS 1 TABLESPOON BUTTERMILK

In a bowl, mix together the flour, salt, and sugar. Add the butter, and use your fingers or a pastry cutter to cut the butter into the flour mixture until coarse and pebbly. Pour in the buttermilk and mix until the dough comes together. Wrap the dough in plastic wrap and gently flatten into a disc. Chill for at least 1 hour before rolling out.

When ready to roll out the dough, lightly flour your work surface and rolling pin. Roll out the dough until about ⅛ inch (3 mm) thick. Cut

into 5-inch (12 cm) rounds. Take dough scraps and knead back together. Roll out to ⅛ inch (3 mm) thick and cut out more rounds. Chill the pie rounds until ready to assemble.

Cinnamon-Sugar MAKES 3 TABLESPOONS

- 1 TABLESPOON GROUND CINNAMON
- 2 TABLESPOONS SUGAR

Stir the cinnamon and sugar together.

Salted Rum Caramel MAKES 1¼ CUPS (300 ML)

- 1 CUP (200 G) SUGAR
- 2 TABLESPOONS DARK RUM
- 6 TABLESPOONS (90 ML) HEAVY CREAM
- 6 TABLESPOONS (85 G) BUTTER
- 1 TEASPOON SEA SALT

In a small pot, combine the sugar and just enough water to make the sugar look like wet sand. Cook over medium heat, without stirring, until the sugar is a deep amber–honey color (when you notice the sugar starting to turn golden on the edges you can gently swirl the pot to prevent it from scorching). Remove from the heat and carefully whisk in the rum followed by the cream. Stir in the butter and salt. Keep warm until ready to serve. The caramel can be stored in the refrigerator for up to 1 week. Rewarm before serving.

Dark Chocolate Tart

with Buckwheat,
Hazelnut,
and Toasted
Meringue

MAKES
1 (8-INCH/
20 CM) TART

THE IDEA FOR THIS TART was never truly my own. It started as a play on s'mores. For a short time, I worked with the wildly talented Chrysta Poulos in Atlanta at Restaurant Eugene and saw her technique for smoked chocolate. I convinced Ben Wheatley, who was the pastry chef at Five & Ten at the time, to make a play on s'mores with smoked chocolate, graham cracker, and toasted meringue. Georgia Kelly, the pastry chef at Greyfield, took the dessert and made it her own by changing the crust to buckwheat, ditching the smoked chocolate, and adding a layer of crunchy hazelnuts. It's truly the best it has ever been.

¾ CUP (90 G) BUCKWHEAT FLOUR

½ CUP (65 G) ALL-PURPOSE FLOUR

3 TABLESPOONS SUGAR

1 TABLESPOON COCOA POWDER

¼ TEASPOON SALT

½ CUP (1 STICK/115 G) COLD BUTTER, *diced small*

2½ TABLESPOONS COLD WATER, *or more as needed*

8 OUNCES (225 G) BITTERSWEET DARK CHOCOLATE (*Valrhona*)

8 OUNCES (225 G) SEMISWEET MILK CHOCOLATE (*Valrhona*)

1¾ CUPS (420 ML) HEAVY CREAM

1 CUP (185 G) HAZELNUT PRALINE (*recipe follows*)

2½ CUPS (600 ML) HONEY MERINGUE (*recipe follows*)

Preheat the oven to 350°F (175°C).

In a food processor, pulse to combine the buckwheat flour, all-purpose flour, sugar, cocoa powder, and salt. Add the butter and pulse until the flour is sandy and the butter is in pea-size chunks. Add the 2½ tablespoons cold water and pulse until the dough comes together. Add more cold water as needed. Remove from the food processor and transfer to an 8-inch (20 cm) tart pan with a removable bottom. Use your hands or a measuring cup to evenly press the dough flat into the sides and bottom of the pan. Refrigerate for 20 minutes before baking.

Place the tart shell on a flat baking sheet and bake until darkened in color and firm to the touch, 15 to 18 minutes. Set aside to cool to room temperature.

While the crust is cooling, make the chocolate filling: Break the chocolate into

smaller pieces and place in a heatproof bowl. In a small pot, bring the cream to a simmer, then pour it over the chocolate and let sit for 2 minutes. Whisk until smooth.

Pour the chocolate filling into the baked crust, filling it up halfway. Sprinkle a thin layer of hazelnut praline over the chocolate, about 12 tablespoons' (140 g) worth. Let cool for 5 minutes in the refrigerator just to lightly set. Pour the remaining chocolate filling over the praline, until just below the crust. Put in the refrigerator to chill until the chocolate is fully set, at least 1 hour or overnight.

Top with dollops of the meringue. Use a kitchen torch to lightly brown the meringue. Garnish with a little more hazelnut praline and serve.

Hazelnut Praline MAKES 1 CUP (185 G)

½ CUP (100 G) SUGAR

1 CUP (115 G) HAZELNUTS, *toasted*

¼ TEASPOON SEA SALT

In a small pot, stir together the sugar and 2 tablespoons water. Cook over medium heat, without stirring, until the sugar begins to caramelize and turn amber in color (when you notice the sugar starting to turn golden on the edges, you can gently swirl the pot to prevent it from scorching). Remove from the heat and stir in the hazelnuts and salt until well coated. Pour onto a sheet pan lined with a Silpat or greased parchment paper and let cool to room temperature. When completely cool, pulse in a food processor until finely chopped. The praline can be made ahead and stored in an airtight container at room temperature for up to 1 month.

Honey Meringue MAKES ABOUT
2½ CUPS (600 ML)

- 2 EGG WHITES
- ½ CUP (100 G) SUGAR
- 1 TABLESPOON HONEY
- 1 TEASPOON SCOTCH WHISKY
- PINCH OF CREAM OF TARTAR

In the heatproof bowl of an electric mixer, whisk together the egg whites, sugar, honey, and Scotch. Place the bowl over a pot of simmering water, making sure the bottom of the bowl does not touch the water, and whisk constantly until the egg whites are hot and the sugar is dissolved, about 4 minutes. Remove bowl from heat. Add the cream of tartar and whisk with the electric mixer on medium-high speed until stiff peaks form.

The meringue can be made a few hours before serving the tart and stored in the refrigerator.

Mitty's Dark and Stormy

SERVES 1

IN HIS LATE SIXTIES, Mitty Ferguson can still out-surf anyone on Cumberland Island. He is effortlessly energetic, managing the marine program at Greyfield and keeping the *Lucy Ferguson*, Greyfield's boat, spotless. Legend has it that during Hurricane Matthew in 2016, Mitty went out at the height of the storm to check on the *Lucy*. He had tied the boat from the dock to a truck parked on higher ground. The damage to the island was substantial. Fernandina had lost half its marina, the national park system had both of its south-end docks damaged, and ravaged boats littered the intracoastal waterway. But the *Lucy* stood, as did Greyfield's dock. Appropriately, Mitty's favorite drink is a Dark and Stormy. Cheers, Mitty.

2   OUNCES (60 ML)
     DARK RUM, *preferably*
     Richland Rum

3   OUNCES (90 ML)
     GINGER BEER, *the*
     spicier the better

½   OUNCE (15 ML)
     LIME JUICE

     ICE CUBES

In a glass, pour the rum, ginger beer, and lime juice. Fill with ice and stir to combine.

HOW TO GRILL A

WHOSE FISH

USE YOUR INSTINCTS

Cooking outside requires you to use your instincts. The size of your fish, the size of your fire, and the proximity of the fish to the fire are all variables that will impact your cooking time. Refer to page 36 for tips on building your fire. Whether choosing to feast alone or serving a crowd, it is an impressive dinner that despite its simplicity feels opulent.

CHOOSING YOUR FISH

- Look for bright eyes and skin that springs back when pushed.
- The smell should be sweet and fresh, like the ocean.
- Ask to have your fish scaled and gutted.
- A fish that is 1½ to 2 pounds (680 to 910 g) will feed four.

PREPPING THE FISH FOR GRILLING

Score the skin of your fish with a sharp knife, making vertical incisions about 2 inches (5 cm) apart. I use my hands to rub olive oil over the skin of the fish. The oil will aid in preventing the fish from sticking to the grill, so use generously. Liberally sprinkle salt over its skin and into the open cavity. Use whole lemongrass and lime to stuff it to impart notes of citrus that mingle with the natural sweetness that lingers from the saltwater.

COOKING THE FISH

Make sure the grate you are grilling on is very clean. I like to gently wipe the grate with oil to prepare it for cooking. The hottest area of the coals should sit just offset of where the fish is grilling. The heat directly under the fish should remain at a consistent medium, allowing the skin to crisp while at the same time evenly cooking the meat. Having an offset high-heat area of coals will give you the ability to cook any side items. Feel free to adjust the coals as needed to maintain a consistent temperature under the fish. Cover the grill while cooking.

FLIPPING THE FISH

When the fish is on the grill, do not move it. The skin will take time to crisp, and if you try to move it around too early, the skin will tear. When the edges begin to look golden, it's ready to flip. Use a large offset spatula and your hand (if you can bear it) to gently flip the fish. If it is cooked through, it will flip easily. If the skin rips a little, don't worry—you can get it perfect on the other side. Cover and continue to cook.

SERVING IT UP

When it's ready, the skin will be crisp and the meat will be firm and opaque. Serve it on a platter whole and use a knife to gently lift the fillets off the bone. Have a little sea salt on the table, some lime wedges, a large bowl of charred pepper chimichurri, and pickled red onion (page 277). Eat outside near the smoldering fire.

CAMPFIRE DINNER

Whole Grilled Vermillion Snapper (page 275), Charred Pepper Chimichurri, Pickled Red Onion, Grilled Hen of the Woods Mushrooms, Pot of Heirloom Beans, Avocados and Espelette SERVES 4

Charred Pepper Chimichurri
MAKES 2 CUPS (480 ML)

- 12 OUNCES (340 G) PEPPERS, *mixed varieties*
- ¼ RED ONION, *diced small*
- 2 CLOVES GARLIC, *minced*
- ¼ CUP (13 G) FINELY CHOPPED FRESH PARSLEY
- 1 TABLESPOON FINELY CHOPPED FRESH OREGANO
- ½ CUP (120 ML) OLIVE OIL
- ¼ CUP (60 ML) RED WINE VINEGAR
- 2 TEASPOONS SALT

Lightly char the peppers on the grill over high heat. The peppers should be soft, but retain some texture. Seed the peppers and small dice them. In a bowl, combine the diced pepper and the remaining ingredients. Any leftover chimichurri can be stored in the refrigerator for up to 5 days.

Pickled Red Onion MAKES 2 CUPS (255 G)

- ½ RED ONION
- ¾ CUP (180 ML) CHAMPAGNE VINEGAR
- 1 TABLESPOON SALT
- 1 SPRIG OF THYME

Peel the onion, remove the ends, and slice thinly, vertically to the root. In a small pot, combine the vinegar, ¾ cup (180 ml) water, and the salt. Bring to a boil. Place the sliced onion and thyme sprig in a nonreactive bowl. Pour the hot vinegar mixture over the onion and place in the refrigerator until cold. Serve cold.

Grilled Hen of the Woods Mushroom
SERVES 4

- 2 BUNCHES HEN OF THE WOODS MUSHROOMS (ABOUT 8 OUNCES/225 G)
- 2 TABLESPOONS OLIVE OIL
- 1½ TEASPOONS SALT

Cut the mushroom bunches in half lengthwise. In a bowl, toss the mushrooms with the oil and salt. Grill the mushrooms over high heat, turning as needed, until lightly charred and cooked through, about 12 minutes.

Pot of Heirloom Beans SERVES 6 TO 8

1   POUND (455 G) DRIED
    HEIRLOOM BEANS (*I like to
    use Rancho Gordo's Santa
    Maria pinquito beans or
    Yellow Indian Woman beans*)

3   TABLESPOONS OLIVE OIL,
    plus more for serving

½   ONION, *minced*

4   CLOVES GARLIC, *minced*

1   SERRANO CHILE, *seeded and
    minced*

1   CUBANELLE PEPPER, *seeded
    and minced*

2   TEASPOONS DRIED OREGANO

2   TABLESPOONS SALT

6   TO 8 SPOONFULS OF CHARRED
    PEPPER CHIMICHURRI (*recipe
    follows*)

Soak the beans in 8 cups (2 L) water in the refrigerator for 12 to 24 hours. Drain the beans.

In a large pot, heat the oil on the stovetop over medium heat. Add the onion, garlic, chile, and Cubanelle pepper. Cook gently for 5 minutes, stirring occasionally. Add the oregano and cook for 1 minute. Add the beans and salt. Cover with 10 cups (2.4 L) water and bring to a boil. Reduce the heat to a simmer, cover, and cook for about 2½ hours, stirring occasionally, until the beans are very tender. The cooking time of your beans will vary depending what kind you use, so keep an eye on them. Taste for seasoning. These can be made ahead and stored in the refrigerator for up to 5 days and then reheated on the grill.

To serve, garnish each serving with a spoonful of the charred pepper chimichurri and a drizzle of olive oil.

Avocados and Espelette SERVES 4 (½ AVOCADO PER PERSON)

2   AVOCADOS

½   TEASPOON SALT

4   TABLESPOONS (60 ML) OLIVE
    OIL

4   HEALTHY PINCHES OF
    ESPELETTE PEPPER

Cut each avocado in half. Remove the pits. Scoop the avocado out of its shell. Place the avocado on a cutting board, pitted side down, and slice each half into 8 thin slices. Transfer to a plate. Season with the salt and olive oil. Garnish with the Espelette pepper and serve immediately.

INDEX

Acknowledgments

Thank you to *The Saltwater Table* team. You carried tables over sandy dunes, endured numerous bug bites, and built fires in the sweltering heat of summer to create a book that is true to the beauty of this magical island. Ben, I could write endlessly to you. This doesn't work without you. You are the most amazing chef, recipe tester, food stylist, and companion any author could hope to work with. Emily, your creative energy and passion for this book is visible in every magnificent photo. Olivia, your enthusiasm and willingness to take on every task handed to you is deeply appreciated. Now, just run to the Inn and grab one more ingredient! Alejandro, your steadfast willingness to run the kitchen in our absence made the making of this book possible. Jessie, your illustrations are as brilliant as the first bright pink grapefruit of the season: refreshing, inspiring, and alluring. Harper, Lyric, and Christopher, no dinner party would be complete without you. Penny, you saw me through the making of this book. I miss you so.

And what good would a dream be if not for those who can listen and see the possibility of creativity. Thank you to Melany Robinson, you are the first person to hear my idea and believe in it. Sarah Smith, your interest and enthusiasm from day one pushed me to write and to express the intangible lure of the southeast coast. I would happily be mistaken for your sister any day. Laura Dozier, you have been a patient guide through this process. You inspire me to be a better writer and a more adventurous traveler. I hope that you will write a book one day so the world can read about your adventures. Deb Wood, your talent and knowing eye organized stacks of documents and piles of photos into a captivatingly beautiful frame. Julia, the Amelia Lady is endlessly inspiring and the only place I want to write. To the Donner, the one I call to read my work, the first person I trust with the words that fall jumbled from my mind onto the daunting blank slate of Microsoft Word. Thank you for being my Mom.

To the Greyfield family, it has been an honor to have the opportunity to share what your family has long recognized as the beauty of preservation of Cumberland Island. Thank you for your continued drive and for giving me the opportunity to create in such a rich environment. Mary Ferguson, you are a champion of ideas—with your encouragement I found my voice as a chef. Mitty Ferguson, you are a role model for all that come to Greyfield—your hard work is only equaled to one thing, your love of scones. Gogo Ferguson and Dave Sayre, the magic on the island hangs heaviest over Godahalu. May there always be enough oysters, tequila, and music. Per and Mouse Lofberg, the beauty of the food in this book would be impossible if not for your kitchen. I would happily cook in your home anytime. Jamie and Liz Ferguson, you inspire all of us to get outside and explore. There is no better grill in the world than the one that sits in your yard. Thank you the staff at Greyfield, past and present, for calling this wild island home.

EDITOR: LAURA DOZIER

DESIGNER: DEB WOOD

PRODUCTION MANAGER: REBECCA WESTALL

LIBRARY OF CONGRESS CONTROL NUMBER: 2018958260

ISBN: 978-1-4197-3815-9

EISBN: 978-1-68335-654-7

PRINTED AND BOUND IN CHINA

10 9 8 7 6 5 4 3

ABRAMS BOOKS ARE AVAILABLE AT SPECIAL DISCOUNTS WHEN PURCHASED
IN QUANTITY FOR PREMIUMS AND PROMOTIONS AS WELL AS FUNDRAISING
OR EDUCATIONAL USE. SPECIAL EDITIONS CAN ALSO BE CREATED TO
SPECIFICATION. FOR DETAILS, CONTACT SPECIALSALES@ABRAMSBOOKS.COM
OR THE ADDRESS BELOW.

ABRAMS The Art of Books
195 Broadway, New York, NY 10007
abramsbooks.com

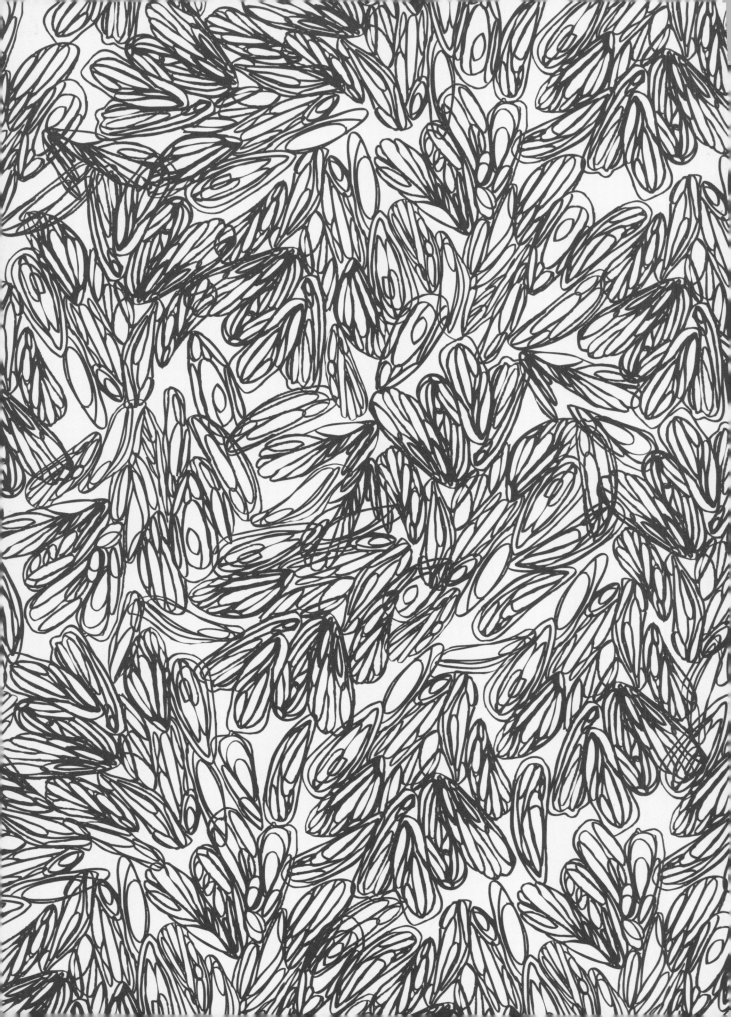